Research-Based Strategies for Literacy Instruction in Grades 3–5

Alice F. Snyder

Kennesaw State University

Kendall Hunt
publishing company
4050 Westmark Drive • P O Box 1840 • Dubuque IA 52004-1840

Cover images:
Letter background © Carlos Caetano, 2009. Used under license
from Shutterstock, Inc.

Teacher with Students © Monkey Business Images, 2009. Used under license
from Shutterstock, Inc.

Contents

CHAPTER ONE: STRATEGIES FOR COMPREHENSION DEVELOPMENT
Background Information and Activities
The Four Cueing Systems..2
    The Marlup Story with Food for Thought Activity 3
Levels of Comprehension Graphic..4
Literacy Comprehension Skills/Strategies Chart (Skills/Strategies Readers Use to
Comprehend Text at Each Level of Comprehension)..5
Activating Background Knowledge (Incorrect and Correct Way) 6
    Three Sisters (Background Knowledge Activity) 7

Best Practices/Instructional Strategies for Teaching Comprehension in Grades 3–5
Background Knowledge/Making Connections 8
    Making Connections Chart..9
Inferential Meaning/Introductory Inferring Lesson................................10
    Sheets for Student Recording of Inferences While Reading....................11
Concept Attainment...12
Talking Drawings..13
    Samples of Talking Drawings 14
Anticipation Guide 16
    Sample Anticipation Guide: *Amos and Boris,* William Steig 17
    Sample Anticipation Guide: *Hatchet,* Gary Paulsen.........................18
    KWL (What I Know—What I Want to Know—What I Learned)..................19
    Blank KWL Chart..20
KWL Plus...21
    Sample KWL Plus: All About Tigers, World Wildlife Fund....................23
ReQuest and Reciprocal Teaching Strategies 24
Questioning the Author—Chart of Queries..27
    Six Teacher Moves While Carrying on a QtA Discussion 28
Directed Reading-Thinking Activity (DR-TA)..29
Imagine, Elaborate, Predict, and Confirm (IEPC) Strategy and Chart............30
Types of Propaganda Techniques (Critical Reading and Viewing) 32
Two Graphic Organizers That Facilitate Comprehension
Problem-Solution Chart 33
Compare-Contrast Chart..34

CHAPTER TWO: STRATEGIES FOR VOCABULARY DEVELOPMENT
Word Knowledge Rating Scale: Explanation with Sample........................36
Word Knowledge Rating Scale for Grades 1–2......................................37
CSSR Flow Chart..38

Best Practices/Instructional Strategies for Teaching Vocabulary in Grades 3–5
Classification/Classification with the Intruder 39
Pictorial Word Webs/Maps 40
Semantic Word Map 41
Concept Circles...42
    Examples of Concept Circles..43
Schwartz Concept of Definition Map 44
    Example of Concept of Definition Map 45
Snyder Word Analysis Map (SWAM) 46
    Examples of Snyder Word Analysis Maps 47
Vocabulary Venn Diagram 49
Word Clusters (explanation and examples) 50
    List of Common Words with 5 or More Meanings 51
Vocabulary Star 52
Semantic Feature Analysis (Word Matrix) with Example......................................53
    Example of Semantic Feature Analysis/Word Matrix (The Solar System) 54
Vocabulary Illustrations/Vocabulary Pictures with examples...............................55
    Examples of Vocabulary Pictures ("mast" and "mansion") 56
Homophone Picture Cards...57
    List of Homophones 58
Word Splash with Example 59
Semantic Impressions with Example 60
Vocab-o-Gram (Predict-o-Gram) 61
    Example of Vocab-o-Gram/Predict-o-Gram 62
Word Expert Cards with Examples 63
Magic Squares 64
    Example of Magic Square on the Ancient World 65
Word Tree Posters 66
Vocabulary Self-Selection Chart (VSS Chart)...67
Thematic Word Walls with example 68
    Samples of Student-Chosen Words for MYSTERY Thematic Word Wall 69
Possible Sentences 70
Contextual Redefinition 71
Analogies (Different Types and Examples of Analogies) 72
Lists of Prefixes, Root Words, and Suffixes, and Their Meanings 73

CHAPTER THREE: STRATEGIES FOR TEACHING PHONICS, SYLLABICATION, DECODING, AND FLUENCY
Assessments to Help Inform Instruction
The Names Test Protocol Sheet (Student's Copy)...82
    The Names Test Record Sheet 83
    The Names Test Sample Student Protocol..84
    Scoring Matrix for the Names Test (p. 1) 85
    Scoring Matrix for the Names Test (p. 2) 86
Stages of Spelling Development..87
Gentry Developmental Spelling Test (Early Years K–8) 88
    Gentry Developmental Spelling Test Scoring Chart..89
Blackburn-Cramp Developmental Writing Scale (Beginning Writers) and Extending
    Writer's Scale (Descriptors for Conventions of Writing) 91

Best Practices/Strategies for Teaching and Developing Phonics, Syllabication, Decoding, and Fluency in Grades 3–5

An Analytic Phonics Lesson Using the Poem "The Tooter" 94

Word Sorting (Grades 3–5) 95

Word Sorting Example (Sound Sort) 96

Inquiry-Based Syllabication Partner Activity: Discovering a Generalization about Dividing Words into Syllables 97

Word Lists One and Two for Inquiry-Based Syllabication Partner Activity.........................98

Sample Inquiry-Based Spelling Lesson: Attacking a Problem of Sound-Alikes.................99

Mystery Word Instructional Strategy for Decoding Multisyllabic Words 102

Sample Mystery Word Exercises 103

Procedures for Syllasearch: An Instructional Strategy for Decoding Multisyllabic Words 104

Sets of Words and Syllables for Syllasearch...107

Elements of Fluency 108

How Punctuation Relates to Comprehension and Fluency 109

Methods and Activities for Teaching Fluency 110

Practice with Sentence Intonation 111

Appendix

Syllabication Generalizations #1–#4 112

Syllabication Generalizations #5–#8 113

Some Spelling "Rules" 114

Rules for Forming Plurals 115

Chapter One

Strategies for Comprehension Development

The Four Cueing Systems

Type	"Definition"	Terms	Uses in the Elementary Grades
Grapho-Phonic	Sound system of English—consists of 44 sounds (phonemes) and more than 500 ways to spell those 44 sounds	• **Phoneme**—smallest unit of sound • **Grapheme**—written representation of a phoneme using 1 or more letters • **Phonetic awareness**—understanding that speech is composed of individual sounds • **Phonics**—teaching sound-symbol correspondences and spelling "generalizations"	• pronouncing words • detecting regional and other dialects • decoding words when reading • using invented spelling • reading & writing alliterations & onomatopoeia • noticing rhyming words • dividing words into syllables
Syntactic	Structural system of English—governs how words are put together to form sentences	• **Syntax**—structure of a sentence; grammar • **Morpheme**—smallest unit of meaning	• adding inflectional endings to words (ing, ed, ies, etc.) • joining words to form compound words • using capitalization & punctuation to designate beginnings & ends of sentences • writing simple, compound, & complex sentences • combining sentences
Semantic	Meaning system of English—focuses on vocabulary as well as understanding what one reads	• **Semantics**—meaning; it's all about the meaning!	• learning the meanings of various words • realizing that some words have multiple meanings • using context clues to determine an unfamiliar word • using dictionary & thesaurus • reading & writing comparisons (metaphors, similies)
Pragmatic	System that varies language according to its uses in social and cultural situations	• **Function**—purpose/why a person uses language • **Standard English**—form used in textbooks & by those in academia, TV news, etc. • **Nonstandard English**—other forms of the language	• altering language to fit specific purposes • reading & writing dialogue in various dialects • comparing standard and nonstandard English

From Tompkins, Gail E. *Literacy for the 21st Century: Teaching Reading and Writing in Grades 4 through 8,* 1/e Published by Allyn and Bacon/Merrill Education, Boston, MA. Copyright © 2004 by Pearson Education. Reprinted by permission of the publisher.

Cueing Systems Demonstration

Directions: Read the following story and then answer the questions.

The Marlup Story

A marlup was poving his kump. Parmily a narg horped some whev in his kump.

"Why did vump horp whev in my frinkle kump?" the marlup jufd the narg.

"Er'm muvvily trungy," the narg grupped. "Er heshed vump norpled whev in your kump. Do vump pove your kump frinkle?"

Now, answer the questions!

1. What did the narg horp in the marlup's kump?

2. What did the marlup juf the narg?

3. Was the narg trungy?

4. How does the marlup pove his kump?

Food for thought . . .

What cueing system(s) helped you read the story and answer the questions?

Which cueing system(s) was/were not at play here? So, were you **really reading**?

Source: Dr. Kenneth Goodman

3

Levels of Comprehension

Using information to express opinions, form new ideas, and evaluate

Applied
(Evaluative/Critical)
Reading beyond the lines

Highest Level

Putting together information, perceiving relationships, making inferences

Interpretive
Reading between the lines

Getting information explicitly from the text

Literal
Reading the lines

Lowest Level

From: Vacca, R.T. & Vacca, J.L. (1996). *Content area reading* (5th Ed.). New York: Harper Collins.

Literacy Comprehension "Skills"/Strategies

Skills/Strategies of Literal Comprehension (Level 1)
- Recalling **explicit** details—who, what, when, where
- Following written directions
- Recalling **explicit** sequence of events
- Identifying **stated** cause-effect relationships
- Comparing and contrasting information
- Identifying **stated** topic and main idea
- Identifying **stated** character traits and actions
- Understanding symbols, abbreviations, and acronyms—translating abbreviated forms of words into meaningful units
- Reading for a **stated** purpose—determining information to be learned from the reading; formulate this information into questions; read to answer the questions

Skills/Strategies of Interpretive Comprehension (Level 2)
- Predicting outcomes—relating elements within a passage to each other in order to determine the result
- Determining **implied** main idea—unstated main topic, idea, theme, or message
- Selecting **implied** cause-effect relationships—interpreting from stated information the implied relationships in an event
- Identifying an **implied** sequence of events—inferring from given information the order of ideas or information
- Interpreting figurative language
- Making inferences (schema-based) depends on BK; text-based, putting together 2+ bits of information from text
- Understanding mood and emotional reactions—responding to imagery or feeling conveyed by the author
- Summarizing information—condensing the information read
- Making generalizations—apply reasoning to given facts in order to make a decision
- Perceiving relationships—identify similarities among ideas in a passage and relate or classify the ideas
- Making connections—Text-to-Text; Text-to-Self; Text-to-World

Skills/Strategies of Applied/Evaluative/Critical Comprehension (Level 3)
- Differentiating between facts and opinions
- Interpreting propaganda techniques—identifying ideas or doctrines promoted by a special group
- Using problem-solving techniques
- Recognizing fallacies in reasoning—recognizing words used to create an illusion, causing illogical or unsound ideas to be relayed
- Identifying relevant and irrelevant information
- Determining reliability of the author
- Evaluating ideas and concepts across texts
- Applying what has been learned to the reader's own purposes—seeing the relationship of what is read to one's own situation and determine possible application
- Evaluating character's actions—judge or evaluate information based on theories, etc.—make moral decisions, judgments
- Placing self in character's shoes and evaluate—i.e., "If you were Brian, would you have . . .? Why or why not?" or "If you were General Lee . . ." or "Given what you know about Robert E. Lee, would you have chosen to fight for the South or the North? Why or why not?"

Activating Background Knowledge

Ineffective Way to Activate Prior Knowledge

"Today we are going to read the article 'Birds in Winter.' How many of you have ever seen birds during the winter? (SR) What are the types of birds that you typically see in the winter months? (SR) How do birds get their food in wintertime?" (SR)

Effective Way to Activate Prior Knowledge (Schema Directed)

"Today we are going to read the article 'Birds in Winter.' But before we read it, I would like you to think about some key ideas that will help you understand what you're about to read. From the title, what do you think this article is going to be about? (Record SRs & discuss). Yes, this article talks about how birds survive during a blizzard. (Write the word *blizzard* on the board. Connect the students' predictions to surviving in a blizzard. Ask 'What is a blizzard?' (SR) Write a sentence on the board using the word *blizzard*, and discuss its meaning.) What do you think it means to survive in a blizzard? What possible problems might birds have surviving during a blizzard?" (Discuss questions; list students' answers on the board, and discuss them. Add your own points to the discussion to extend and clarify.)

Example responses:

1. A blizzard is a terrible snowstorm with very high winds.

2. Birds could have many problems surviving in a blizzard, such as getting food, not freezing to death, finding water to drink, finding a place to sleep that is protected from the wind.

Use your background knowledge as you read the poem and answer the questions below.

Three Sisters

With hocked gems financing him
Our hero bravely defied all scornful laughter
That tried to prevent his scheme.

Your eyes deceive, he said;
An egg, not a table
Correctly typifies this unexpected domain.

Now three sturdy sisters sought proof
Forging along sometimes through calm vastness
Yet more often over turbulent peaks and valleys.

Days became weeks
As many doubters spread
Fearful rumors about the edge.

At last from nowhere
Welcome winged creatures appeared
Signifying momentous success.

Now, answer the questions below:

1. What was hocked?

2. How many sisters were there?

3. How long were they gone?

4. Who or what appeared at the end of the poem?

5. Find three describing words. _____, _____, _____

6. Who was the implied main character in the poem?

7. From your own knowledge base, what do you know about him?

Where in the poem did you achieve comprehension? How?

From: *Journal of Experimental Psychology,* Vol 88 (2), May 1971, by D. James Dooling and Roy Lachman.

Background Knowledge
(Prior Knowledge, Making Connections)

Competent readers activate background knowledge (BK or PK) and make personal connections to text automatically. Inexperienced or struggling readers must be taught in explicit ways to make connections by using texts that they can connect to their own experiences. For those students who may have limited background experiences or who may have trouble making connections to their own lives, the teacher must provide these experiences for them and then model, through think-alouds, how connections are made. There are three types of connections:

Text to Self (T-S)—the child connects the text to his/her own personal experiences
Text to Text (T-T)—the child connects the text to another text he/she has read or viewed
Text to World (T-W)—the child connects the text with his/her own general knowledge about the world and how things "work" in the world around him or her

An Introductory Lesson about Making Connections (Background Knowledge)

Materials—any picture book to which the teacher has a personal connection and can make connections with other texts or connections with general knowledge about the world; post-it notes, pens & pencils, the board. [You can also choose books that focus on only one type of connection at a time. For example, you can choose a book for one lesson that you and the students can make only Text-to-Self connections, then focus a different lesson on a text that you and the students can make Text-to-Text connections, etc.]

Setting the Stage—Ask the students to tell you what Background Knowledge means. After a brief discussion, explain what it means and give examples. Intro the book by sharing with them that the book reminds you of your childhood, family, etc. Briefly discuss the plot of the book.

Shared Reading—Read the book aloud to the students. As you read, think aloud about how certain parts of the book remind you of something. Demonstrate how to write notes on the post-it notes as you remember things. Once the students seem to understand and offer their own connections, give them a post-it note to write their own connections, making sure they put their names on the post-its. Encourage them to make connections for the rest of the book.

Conclusion and Follow-up—Go back and reread the connections that were made. Re-emphasize why it is so important to make connections while reading. After introducing the three types of connections, go back to the connections made during this lesson and label each with what type of connection it is, T-T, T-S, or T-W. Place them on the three-column **Making Connections Chart** (see next page).

Record the connections that you make while you read on the chart below using the correct note pattern.

Making Connections Chart

(created by Alice Snyder)

Text-to-Text	Text-to-Self	Text-to-World

Inferential Meaning

Inferring meaning is the foundation of comprehension. We make inferences in our lives all the time. Inferring is about reading facial expressions, body language, voice tone, as well as written text. One basic, introductory lesson in making inferences involves helping children understand their own and others' feelings by responding to verbal clues. In a higher level lesson, students may make inferences from facts or quotes in the text. As with other comprehension skills and strategies, students must be explicitly taught to make inferences. They must be given multiple opportunities to practice the skill with a variety of texts during guided reading or whole class discussion of content area reading. As students become more proficient with the skill, they may practice independently or during literature circle groups. Some texts that could be used to develop inferring are: *Dandelion* by Eve Bunting, *Rose Blanche* by Roberto Innocenti, *Tight Times* by Barbara Shook Hasen, and *Teammates* by Peter Golenbock.

Introductory Inferring Lesson

Purpose: To help students better understand their own feelings and to introduce inferential thinking

Resources: Large index cards with feeling words written on them. Card is pinned or taped on the back of one student volunteer who doesn't know what it says.

Procedure: After discussing feelings, the teacher chooses one feeling word and tapes it to the student volunteer's back. Other students form a large circle around the student volunteer. Student volunteer slowly turns around so that the others can see the word. The teacher asks the class to give clues for the word by starting with "I felt that way when . . ." For example, for the word **frustrated**, the students might give clues like:

- I felt that way when the computer shut down in the middle of my project and I lost all of my work.

- I felt that way when I could not solve a puzzle.

After 4 or 5 students have a chance to give a clue, the teacher asks the volunteer if he/she can infer what the feeling is. If the student answers correctly, the teacher asks him how he made the inference without actually hearing the word. If the volunteer answers incorrectly, others continue with clues until the volunteer answers correctly or the teacher provides assistance. The game continues with a few more student volunteers and new feeling words are used.

Source: Harvey, S. & Goudvis, A. (2000). *Strategies that work*. York, ME: Stenhouse [pp. 105–106].

Two Examples of Sheets for Student Recording of Inferences While Reading

Name _____   Date _____

Quote or Picture from the Text	Inference Made

Name _____   Date _____

Facts Taken from the Text	Inference Made

Source: Harvey, S. & Goudvis, A. (2000). *Strategies that work*. York, ME: Stenhouse [p. 278].

Concept Attainment

Concept Attainment is an inquiry-based activity suited for grades 1–5 that takes place prior to beginning a new book or when introducing a new topic or theme to be studied in one of the content areas. Based on the work of Jerome Bruner, concept attainment helps learners develop understandings about conceptual knowledge by finding commonalities among ideas and concepts. It can be done as an individual, partner, or small group activity, although I have found it works best when done in partners. The teacher determines what overlying theme or topic is being presented in the upcoming text. Then the teacher composes about six example sentences that depict that theme or topic in a variety of contexts and about four non-example sentences that do not depict that theme or topic. (Pictures or objects can be used as well in place of sentences, depending on the age of the students). These sets of ten sentences are cut out and given to each pair of students along with two cards, one with a "Yes" and one with a "No." The teacher does not give specific directions to the students other than at first telling them "Read the statements and decide which ones should go under the 'yes' column and which ones should go under the 'no' column, based on what they may have in common." After giving the students a few minutes to read and ponder over the statements, the teacher asks "Does anyone have a guess as to what one of the yes statements might be?" The teacher takes only one volunteer. The student gives the number of the statement and reads it orally to the class. The teacher then rereads the statement and says "That's a yes statement" or "That's actually a no statement." "Now that you have one clue, continue discussing the rest of the statements and see what you think now." Give the students a couple more minutes to ponder, then ask "Does anyone have a guess as to what another one of the yes statements might be?" The teacher takes one more volunteer's guesses and gives the appropriate feedback. Then after a couple more minutes, the teacher asks, "Does anyone know what a 'no' statement might be?" The teacher takes one volunteer's possible no statement and gives the appropriate feedback. The teacher gives a few more minutes for the students to manipulate their statements and think about how all the yes statements may go together. After this, the teacher asks the students if anyone might know what all the yes statements have in common . . . what concept or theme they are all about. Students give their responses and their reasoning for their responses. Throughout this discovery-inquiry activity, the teacher does not give clues to the students to help them. This activity is designed to allow students to attain the concept or theme to be studied on their own with peer help. Below are examples* of concept attainment statements for the concept of **loyalty:**

1. Susie wanted to hang around with the popular group, but she stayed with her shy, seldom-noticed, best friend, Anne. (Y)

2. When Bullwinkle and Rocky got in trouble for smashing the pumpkins on Natasha Street on Halloween, Sylvester told the police that Rocky was the mastermind of the plot in order to receive a lighter punishment. (N)

3. There was always a large crowd that attended the Browns' football games no matter how badly they played. (Y)

4. Luke, a Canadian goose, and his mate, Lucy, could always be seen together in the summer in Ohio on farmer Jones's pond and in the winter in the swamplands of South Carolina. (Y)

5. After the election, many of the winning democratic candidates changed their party affiliation. (N)

6. The captured soldier divulged military secrets in exchange for his freedom. (N)

7. When a cavalry unit came to relieve John Dunbar from his post, John stayed with his adopted Sioux tribe and was hunted down like a criminal. (Y)

8. Even though Mr. and Mrs. Tickles were divorced, Mrs. Tickles would not say bad things about her ex-husband when friends and family put him down. (Y)

9. The odds were against Funny Side on winning the Triple Crown, but horse racing fans bet on him winning the race. (Y)

10. When the ship went down, many wives chose to stay on board with their husbands rather than get on the lifeboats. (Y)

---

*Example statements intended for teacher education students for purpose of demonstrating Concept Attainment strategy.

Talking Drawings

Purpose: To help readers use prior knowledge to improve their recall and comprehension of narrative and expository texts. Talking Drawings help the reader create a mental image before and after reading as he/she constructs meaning. It offers the reader the opportunity to draw what he/she visualizes prior to reading, using the reader's prior knowledge and understanding about the concept or topic and again after reading, when the reader constructs another drawing that shows his/her learned knowledge.

Audience: Elementary, middle, and secondary students

Before Reading

Step One: Tell students to close their eyes and imagine topic X, event X or the character X that will be studied or read about. After a few seconds, ask them to open their eyes and draw what they see in their minds.

Step Two: Students share their drawings with one or two other students, talking about and analyzing their drawing, explaining why they drew what they did.

Step Three: Students may volunteer to share their drawings with the entire class in which they may share personal experiences and information sources that came into play when they drew their pictures. A concept map may be written on the board that reflects the class's contributions.

During Reading

Step Four: Students read the assigned textbook pages or section, or assigned article, or narrative text, keeping their drawings in mind as they read.

After Reading

Step Five: After the text has been read, engage the class (or small groups) in discussion of the text, article, or narrative text, asking students to create a new drawing based on new understandings gained from their reading.

Step Six: Students share and/or compare their before and after reading drawings, discussing their changes and reasons for any changes made. They are encouraged to revisit the text to specific passages that support their changes.

Step Seven: Students are then encouraged to write about how their before and after drawings have changed, and any new understandings they have developed throughout the process.

Step Eight: As an optional step, students may then conduct further research on the topic on the internet or other sources.

McConnell, S. (1992/1993). Talking drawings: A strategy for assisting learners. *Journal of Reading, 36* (4), 260–269.

Talking Drawings Sample Narrative Lesson

1. Close your eyes and think about <u>a wolf</u>. Now, open your eyes and draw what you saw.

2. Read/Listen to the selection *Wolf* by Becky Bloom, then draw a second picture to show what you learned.

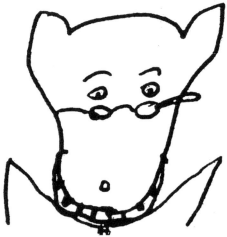

3. In the space below, tell what you have changed about your before and after pictures.

The wolf in this story isn't like the one in Little Red Riding Hood. He starts off mean and tries to scare everyone. Then, he watches the cow, pig and duck love to read. He wants to impress his friends. So, he decides he better learn to read, too.

Talking Drawings Sample
Expository Lesson

1. Close your eyes and think about <u>volcanoes</u>. Now, open your eyes and draw what you saw.

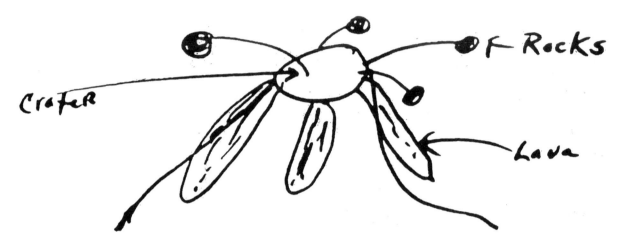

2. Read your selection on "Volcanoes" from Chapter 12 then draw a second picture to show what you learned.

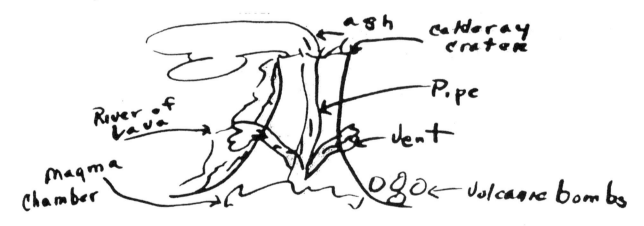

3. In the space below, tell what you have changed about your before and after pictures.

At first, I only drew the mountain and the lava coming down the sides. From our textbook and the video, I learned that there is a magma chamber inside that causes the eruption to flow through the pipe and out the caldera, the huge opening at the top. There is a river of lava that flows down the side of the mountain. Ash and volcanic bombs can be seen around the volcano.

From Karen D. Wood, D. Bruce Taylor, *Literacy Strategies Across the Subject Areas: Process-Oriented Blackline Masters for the K–12 Classroom,* 2/e. Published by Allyn and Bacon/Merrill Education, Boston, MA. Copyright © 2006 by Pearson Education. Reprinted by permission of the publisher.

Anticipation Guide

Purpose: Also called a Reaction Guide or Prediction Guide, its purpose is to help the reader make predictions about what the upcoming text will be about. In addition, the teacher is able to get an idea about what conceptual understandings (or misunderstandings) the reader has about the topic to be read. It prepares the reader for reading by asking him/her to read a series of generic statements that are likely to stimulate the reader's thinking, then make a decision to either agree/disagree, choose a yes/no response, or true/false response.

Audience: Anticipation Guides can be used for elementary, middle, and secondary students.

Teacher Preparation: Choose a story, textbook chapter, or selection from a newspaper, nonfiction text, essay, etc. that conveys key content and/or concepts to be studied. Develop about five to eight generic statements, depending on grade level, that reflect the key concepts discussed in the text. Type them on a handout (can also put them in overhead transparency format or PowerPoint) and provide a copy for each student.

Before Reading

Step One: If a transparency or PowerPoint is prepared, display the Anticipation Guide as well as hand out individual guides to each child. Tell students that the guide is a device that helps them combine what they know about a topic or concept with what they can predict about the text.

Step Two: Students read each statement and think about whether they agree or disagree with the statements or think the statements are true or false, etc. Tell students to circle agree or disagree, true or false, yes or no, depending on how the guide is designed. You may decide to have students complete their guides with a partner so that they may engage in discussion before making a decision about each statement. Tell students that the guide will not be graded.

During Reading

Step Three: Students read, listen to, or view the text using the statements as a means to guide them through the key concepts in the text.

After Reading

Step Four: After the text is read, the students are encouraged to revisit their Anticipation Guide as they validate or re-evaluate their original answers, based on what they have read. Students can respond as a class, in small groups, or individually to show if they agreed or disagreed with the statements after reading the text. This opportunity to discuss is important to developing conceptual understandings and gives the teacher insights into their understandings as well. Misconceptions can then be discussed and clarified.

Note: Extended Anticipation Guide: Anticipation Guides can be *extended* by asking students to write a sentence explaining why they think each statement is true or false or why they agree or disagree with the statement, etc. Another idea is to have students, after reading, go back and re-evaluate their original responses and find evidence in the text to back up the correct responses.

Source: Herber, H.L. (1970). *Teaching reading in the content areas.* Upper Saddle River, NJ: Prentice Hall.

Anticipation Guide

Amos and Boris, by William Steig

Read each statement and circle **Agree** if you agree with the statement and **Disagree** if you do NOT agree with the statement.

1. Whales and mice are very different kinds of animals.

   Agree   Disagree

2. Mice do not like the water.

   Agree   Disagree

3. Whales are dangerous, mean creatures.

   Agree   Disagree

4. Whales are fish.

   Agree   Disagree

5. Mice are mammals.

   Agree   Disagree

6. Best friends will do anything to help each other when one is in trouble.

   Agree   Disagree

Steig, W. (1971). *Amos and Boris.* New York: Farrar, Straus and Giroux.

Anticipation Guide

Hatchet, by Gary Paulsen

Read each statement and circle TRUE if you agree with the statement and FALSE if you disagree with the statement. Then read the book *Hatchet.* When finished, go back and re-evaluate your original thinking, based on the story.

1. A 13-year-old boy can fly a small airplane by himself.

   True   False

2. A person would need more than just a hatchet in order to survive in the wilderness alone for many weeks.

   True   False

3. Moose are friendly animals.

   True   False

4. Mosquitoes only live in damp, warm environments.

   True   False

5. The only way to kill small game is to shoot it.

   True   False

6. If you were stranded on a desert island, the most important thing you would need to survive is fire.

   True   False

7. If you come across a bear, the best thing to do is run away.

   True   False

8. The only time a wild animal will attack a person or other animal is when it's protecting its young.

   True   False

Paulsen, G. (1987). *Hatchet.* New York: Alladdin Paperbacks.

KWL

Purpose: KWL helps determine students' prior knowledge and prior experiences before, during, and after reading to increase their comprehension and recall of expository material. It is a schema-based brainstorming activity that organizes not only what students already know, but also what they want to learn about a topic prior to reading and instruction, and what they learned as a result of reading and instruction. In a standard KWL chart, the **K** represents what students already **know** about the topic, the **W** stands for what they **want** to know or learn more about the topic which guides their reading, and **L** stands for what they **learned** in the course of reading and instruction.

Audience: Elementary, Middle, and Secondary Students

Before Reading

Step One: Display the KWL chart on the overhead, on large chart paper, or on the board. Provide an individual KWL chart to each child. Explain what each column represents.

Step Two: Ask students to think about everything they know about the topic the class is going to be studying. As each student provides a response about what he or she knows, write the child's response under the **K** column in the child's exact words. In parentheses, write the child's name after the response. In this way, you are conveying that the child's response is worthy of noting. If the response is long, you may ask "If I understand you correctly, are you saying . . .?" If the child agrees, then a shortened version may be written with the child's name placed after the response as indicated. If students have their own copies of the KWL, they write the responses accordingly.

Step Three: Next, ask the students what they would like to learn about the topic they are going to be studying. Write these contributions under the **W** column, indicating the name of the child who contributed each statement. The teacher may add a couple questions or items as well to help emphasize important concepts. These questions serve as purposes for reading to guide them as they read for information.

During Reading

Step Four: Tell students to read the assigned text(s), referring to the **W** column as a means to guide them. (Not only does the KWL work well with material that is read, but also with other types of texts, such as videos, experiments, lectures, and others.)

After Reading

Step Five: Once students have read the text, ask them to brainstorm what they learned and write their responses under the **L** column of the chart. Remember to write the child's name after his/her contribution. The teacher may need to prompt for additional key concepts that children may not mention.

From: Ogle, D. S. (1986). K-W-L group instructional strategy. In A. S. Palincsar, D. S. Ogle, B. F. Jones, & E. G. Carr (Eds.), *Teaching reading as thinking* (Teleconference Resource Guide, pp. 11–17). Alexandria, VA: Association for Supervision and Curriculum Development.

KWL Chart

What I (We) Know	What I (We) Want to Know	What I (We) Learned

KWL Plus

Purpose: The KWL Plus helps determine students' prior knowledge and prior experiences before, during, and after reading to increase their comprehension and recall of expository material. It is a schema-based, brainstorming activity that organizes not only what students already know, but also what they want to learn about a topic prior to reading and instruction, and what they learned as a result of reading and instruction. In a standard KWL chart, the **K** represents what students already **know** about the topic, the **W** stands for what they **want** to know or learn more about the topic which guides their reading, and **L** stands for what they **learned (and still need to know)** in the course of reading and instruction. With the **KWL Plus** however, students take the KWL one step further by **categorizing** the information they listed in the **L** column. From there, students are encouraged, with the teacher's assistance, to create a graphic organizer of the categorized information.

Audience: Elementary, Middle, and Secondary Students

Before Reading

Step One: Display the KWL chart on the overhead, on large chart paper, or on the board. Provide an individual KWL chart to each child. Explain what each column represents.

Step Two: Ask students to think about everything they know about the topic the class is going to be studying. As each student provides a response about what he or she knows, write the child's response under the **K** column in the child's exact words. In parentheses, write the child's name after the response. In this way, you are conveying that the child's response is worthy of noting. If the response is long, you may ask "If I understand you correctly, are you saying . . .?" If the child agrees, then a shortened version may be written with the child's name placed after the response as indicated above. If students have their own copies of the chart, they will write the responses accordingly.

Step Three: Next, ask the students what they would like to learn about the topic they are going to be studying. Write these contributions under the **W** column, indicating the name of the child who contributed each statement. The teacher may add a couple questions or items as well to help emphasize important concepts. These questions will serve as purposes for reading to guide them as they read for information.

During Reading

Step Four: Tell students to read the assigned text(s), referring to the **W** column as a means to guide them. (Not only does the KWL work well with material that is read, but also with other types of texts, such as videos, experiments, lectures, and others.)

Source: Carr, E. & Ogle, D.M. (1987). K-W-L-Plus: A strategy for comprehension and summarization. *Journal of Reading, 30*, 626–631.

After Reading

Step Five: Once students have read the text, ask them to brainstorm what they learned and write their responses under the **L** column of the chart. Remember to write the child's name after his/her contribution. The teacher may need to prompt for additional key concepts that children may not mention.

Step Six: Ask students to think about how they may categorize the information listed in the **"What I learned and still need to know"** column. Guide students in this process by modeling a few examples. You may do this by using letter or pictorial symbols to represent categories, then have students categorize the information accordingly. As a class or in small groups, organize the categories into a semantic web.

Writing Stage

Step Seven: Put students into pre-assigned groups or pairs. Ask them to choose one of the categories and write a paragraph about the information in that category. They may refer to the text if needed. Pairs or groups may share their paragraphs with the class when each group is finished. The teacher may want to model, through the think-aloud process, how to take information on a graphic organizer and convert it to a cohesive paragraph. Overall, this activity is a great way to demonstrate to students how they can read for information, then organize what they learned into a graphic organizer that can assist them in the process of writing a report or other informational forms of writing.

KWL Plus—
All About Tigers

1. Whole class/small group contributions (steps 2–6)

What I Know	What I Want to Learn	What I Learned and Still Need to Know
• They live in jungles (Tim) • They have sharp teeth (Susie) • They look a lot like house cats (Jamila) • They hunt for their food (Roberto)	• What animals do they hunt for to eat? (Yung) • How big can tigers get? (Erika) • How do they teach their babies to hunt? (Maria) • What countries in the world do they live? (teacher)	• live in jungle forests (Tim) **[L]** • Western India and Southeast Asia (Tim) **[L]** • every tiger has different stripes—none look alike (Jamila) **[A]** • hunt deer, antelopes, wild pigs (John) **[E]** • thick pads on feet to hunt silently (Roberto) **[A]** • mother teaches cubs how to hunt and get along in the jungle (Maria) **[B]** • also eat fish, birds, berries, eggs (Yung) **[E]** • front teeth—fangs—used to bite and tear meat (Susie) **[A]** • male tigers can weigh 700 pounds & be 10 ft. long (Erika) **[A]** • like to swim when it's hot (Maria) **[B]** • sleep during the day (Tim) **[B]** • hunt at night (Roberto) **[B]** • Stripes hide them in shadows (Jamila) **[A]**

2. Class or Group Created Semantic Map (Step 6)

What They Eat
• deer, antelopes, wild pigs
• fish, birds, berries, eggs

Tigers

Where They Live
• jungle forests
• Western India and Southeast Asia

Their Behavior
• mother teaches cubs how to hunt and get along in the jungle
• like to swim when it's hot
• sleep during the day
• hunt at night

What They Look Like
• different stripes—none look alike
• thick pads on feet to hunt silently
• front teeth—fangs—used to bite and tear meat
• male tigers can weigh 700 lbs. & be 10 ft. long
• stripes hide them in shadows

3. Summary for "Appearance/What They Look Like" (Step 7)

Tigers are very large wild cats. They look like house cats. Male tigers can weigh up to 700 pounds and can measure ten feet long. Just like people, no two tigers look alike. Every tiger has different stripes. These stripes help to hide them in shadows. They have thick pads on their feet that help them hunt quietly. They also have large front teeth called fangs that are used to bite and tear meat.

World Wildlife Fund, 1988, Determined Productions, Inc., USA.

ReQuest Instructional Strategy
(Reciprocal Questioning)

Reciprocal Questioning (Manzo, 1969) enhances comprehension through a process of back and forth questioning between the teacher and the students. It is based on the premise that 1) asking the right question is just as important as knowing the correct answer, especially when the purpose of reading is to gain information from text, and 2) the teacher is a powerful model for student behavior. Therefore, if students are exposed to an excellent model, i.e., a teacher who asks good questions about text, then the students will assume similar questioning strategies and begin to ask good "teacher-type" questions when they read.

MODELING IS THE KEY TO FACILITATING LEARNING AND ALLOWING THE LEARNER TO BECOME AN INDEPENDENT READER AND LEARNER!!

1. Teacher assigns short section of text for students (and teacher) to read silently; teacher turns book over and invites students to ask "teacher type" questions about the section of text just read; teacher answers questions as well as possible; then students turn book over; teacher asks follow-up questions about that same portion of text that was just read to call attention to other important information in that section; students answer questions

2. Teacher assigns another short section of text for students to read silently; teacher turns book over; students ask teacher questions about that portion of text that was just read; teacher answers questions

3. Teacher assigns another short section of text for all to read silently; students turn text over; teacher asks questions, ensuring that questions tie in to those from previous segment in order to help students perceive the importance of integration and accumulation of knowledge; students answer

4. Teacher assigns another short section; teacher turns text over; students ask questions; teacher answers

5. Procedure continues until students are able to predict what is going to happen, what other information they are going to obtain, or what they need to do to complete activities or exercises. ("Based on what we've read so far, what do you think the rest of the chapter will be about?", etc.) Procedure can also continue until chapter or lesson in text is completed.

Categories of Questions for ReQuest Strategy

1. Text-explicit questions—questions can be answered directly from the text

2. Questions that link to common knowledge or background knowledge and can be reasonably answered ("Based on what you know about . . . what . . .? how . . .? where would you . . .?)

3. Questions for which the teacher does not expect a correct answer but for which the teacher can provide some information ("Have you ever seen a . . .?)

4. Questions that invite the students to ponder about because neither the teacher nor the text is likely to provide a "correct" answer but are still worth consideration or discussion ("I wonder how . . .")

5. Questions that can be answered but not from the text being read; further reference is needed in order to answer the question

6. Questions that require translation, such as from one level of abstraction to another, from one symbolic form or verbal form to another ("In your own words, . . .")

Manzo, A. (1969). The ReQuest procedure. *Journal of Reading, 13,* 123–126.

Reciprocal Teaching (RT)

Reciprocal Teaching (Palinscar & Brown, 1984) can be used for narrative and expository texts. It takes place in a small group setting. Each group member serves as a leader who follows a 4-step process with a predetermined section of the text. After leading the group through the 4 steps with the section of text, then another group member becomes leader and he/she goes through process with the next predetermined section of text, and so on, until the text has been read and each group member has served in the leader role. Below is the list of the four step sequence that each leader proceeds through as he/she leads the group through the active reading process with each section of the assigned text.

Four Steps (Sequence) Used in RT

1. **Prediction:** Activate prior knowledge and set purpose for reading. Students then read the section of the text silently.

2. **Questioning:** Focus on main ideas and check for understanding. Leader asks question that pulls main idea(s) of section. Leader asks group if they have any questions about the reading. Together, the group constructs meaning.

3. **Seeking clarification:** Ensure that readers are actively engaged and check for understanding. The leader asks group if there is anything about the section that is still confusing to them. Group collaboratively clarifies by seeking dictionary, other resources, revisits text, etc.

4. **Summarization:** Require students to pay attention to critical content. Leader summarizes the section of text read.

Palinscar, A. & Brown, A. (1984). Reciprocal teaching of comprehension fostering and comprehension monitoring activities. *Cognition and Instruction, 1*(2), 117–175.

Questioning the Author
A Questioning Strategy That Engages Interactive Reading

GOAL	QUERIES
• Initiate discussion	• What is the author trying to say? • What is the author's message? • What is the author talking about?
• Help students focus on the author's message	• That's what the author says, but what does it mean?
• Help students link information	• How does that connect with what the author already told us? • How does that fit in with what the author already told us? • What information has the author added here that connects to or fits in with_____?

• Identify difficulties with the way the author has presented information	• Does that make sense?
	• Is that said in a clear way?
	• Did the author explain that clearly?
	  • Why or why not?
	  • What's missing?
	  • What do we need to figure out or find out?

• Encourage students to refer back to the text either because they've misinterpreted a statement or to help them recognize that they've made an inference	• Did the author tell us that? • Did the author give us the answer to that?

• Encourage students to recognize plot development	• What do you think the author is getting at here?
	  • What's going on?
	  • What's happening?
	• What has the author told us now?

• Motivate students to consider how problems are addressed or resolved	• So, how did the author settle that for us? • How did the author work that out for us?

• Help students recognize author's technique	• How has the author let you know that something has changed in the story?
	• How is the author painting a picture here?
	• How did the author let you see something/feel something/smell something?
	• What has the author told us that (character's name) doesn't know?
	• What is the author doing here?
	  • How did the author create humor/suspense/sadness, etc?
	  • Why do you suppose the author used foreshadowing/flashback, etc?

• Prompt students to consider characters' thoughts and actions	• How do things look for (character's name) now? • What is the author trying to tell us about _____ (character's name)?
• Prompt students to predict what a character might do	• Given what the author has already told us, how do you think (character's name) will handle the situation?

Beck, I.L., & McKeown, M.G. (2006). *Improving Comprehension with Questioning the Author: A Fresh and Enhanced View of a Proven Approach.* New York: Scholastic, Inc.

Six Teacher Moves While Carrying on a QtA (Questioning the Author) Discussion

Marking—Teacher highlights a student's comment or idea that's important to the meaning being built

> **Ex:** "As Susan said, Amos didn't think he was going to be able to last very long treading water in the middle of the ocean."

Turning Back—Teacher turns students' attention back to text to get more information, fix up a misreading, or clarify their thinking

> **Ex:** "If you look back on page 8, it says 'But it evaded his grasp and went bowling along under full sail, and he never saw it again.' So Amos couldn't catch up with his boat because the sails were open and the ocean breeze and currents carried it away from him."

Revoicing—Teacher helps students clearly express what they are trying to say

> **Ex:** "If I'm understanding you correctly, John, you're saying that even though Amos was upset with Boris for diving underwater without warning Amos, Amos didn't stay mad at Boris very long because he knew that Boris saved his life? Is that what you meant?"

Modeling—Teacher shows how she may go about creating meaning, how she clarifies a difficult passage, draws a conclusion, visualizes a complex process, uses context to determine word meaning

> **Ex:** "Hmmm, I'm not sure what the word 'sound' means here. I know what a sound is, but in this sentence, 'From then on, whenever Boris wanted to **sound**, he warned Amos in advance and got his okay, and whenever he **sounded**, Amos took a swim.' the word is used as a verb because of 'to sound' and 'he sounded.' I know that whales make sounds, but that alone wouldn't make Amos go somersaulting into the water. I can look at the picture and here I see Boris diving into the water and Amos taking a tumble off Boris's back, so maybe when a whale **sounds,** that means he dives into the water. I'll look it up in the dictionary to make sure I'm right."

Annotating—Teacher fills in missing information from discussion but is important to understanding key ideas; may be information author left out (inferencing)

> **Ex:** "Mice can swim, but they can't swim for long periods of time."

Recapping—Teacher highlights key points and summarizes

> **Ex:** "This story is about a mouse named Amos that loves the ocean so much that he studies navigation and builds a boat that he takes out onto the ocean to explore the world. After falling off his boat, he is saved by a whale named Boris who takes him back to his homeland. After discovering that they're both mammals and spending time together, they became the best of friends. Years later, Boris was washed ashore onto Amos's homeland by a fierce hurricane. Amos tells Boris he will help him, but Boris doesn't know how a small mouse like Amos can help a huge whale like he is. But Amos goes and gets two large elephants that roll Boris back into the water. The two old friends say good-bye, not knowing if they'll ever see each other again."

Adapted from: Beck, I.L., McKeown, M.G., Hamilton, R.L. & Kucan, L. (1997). *Questioning the author: An approach for enhancing student engagement with text.* Newark, DE: International Reading Association.

Examples created by Alice Snyder using the book *Amos and Boris,* 1971, by William Steig (Farrar, Straus, and Giroux Publishers, New York).

Directed Reading-Thinking Activity (DR-TA)

DR-TA consists of a **sequence of three questions** that can frequently be asked in the course of a discussion during guided reading or with content area instruction during discussion of a text. The three questions, in order, are:

1. "**What** do you think?" or "What do you think will happen next?"
2. "**Why** do you think so?" or "Why do you think this will happen?"
3. "Can you **prove** it?" or "What else might happen?" (Most important here is to have the reader provide proof to support his/her answers to #1 and #2 with evidence from the text or prior learning)

For **narrative texts**, it's important that students be given opportunities to read silently, then go through the sequence of the underlined questions above during the course of the grand conversation. At the END of the grand conversation, the sequence of questions that are not underlined above can be asked regarding the chapter coming up, the one(s) not read yet, so that students are given opportunities to predict.

For **expository texts,** teachers can follow the following steps as they implement DR-TA:

1. Identify the purpose of the reading. Begin with a quick survey of the title, subheadings, illustrations, etc. Ask predicting question **"What do you think this chapter/section will be about?"** (1) Record predictions on board and ask **"Why do you think so?"** (2) Encourage guided discussion.
2. Adjust the rate and amount of reading (each predetermined chunk to be read silently) to the purposes and nature of the material.
3. Ask students to read silently to that predetermined logical stopping point in the text. Use a 3x5 or 5x8 index card for students to place on the page so as not to read ahead before answering questions. Observe the reading (of individual students to see amount of difficulty they may have with comprehension, vocabulary, etc.).
4. Guide reader–text interactions. This can be done during discussion time. Students are encouraged to rework predictions as they read and write down revisions.
5. Extend learning through discussion, further reading, additional study, or writing.
   a. after reading, students are asked if predictions were inaccurate, if they had to revise or reject any predictions, how they knew revision was necessary, and what their new predictions were
   b. small group discussion is useful at this time
   c. teacher asks open-ended questions that encourage generalization and application relevant to students' predictions and significant concepts presented
6. Ask proof from students for their predictions, ideas. **"How do you know that?" "Why did you think so?" What made you think that way?"** (3) Students should share passages, sentences, etc., for further proof.

From: Stauffer, R.G. (1969). *Directing reading maturity as a cognitive process.* New York: Harper Row.

Imagine, Elaborate, Predict, and Confirm (IEPC)

IEPC is a strategy used to promote readers' use of visual imagery as a way to enrich their understanding of information that is read, listened to, or viewed. It increases their comprehension and recall by using visual imagery to predict events in a text. The teacher begins by modeling how to imagine a scene, then add details, followed by how to predict a possible story line for the text. After students read, they go back to confirm or readjust their original predictions. The four components of IEPC are:

- **Imagine:** Close your eyes and imagine the scene. Share your thinking with your partner. Now share it with the whole class.

- **Elaborate:** Think of details that are surrounding the scene you've imagined in your head. How do you think the characters feel? What are similar experiences? Describe the scene. What do you see? What do you feel? What do you hear? What do you smell?

- **Predict:** Use what you've imagined to predict what might happen in the story (characters, events, setting, problem, resolution, etc.)

- **Confirm:** While you are reading, and after reading the selection, keep your original predictions in your mind. Were they true, false, or were they not explained in the text? Adjust your original predictions to go along with the text.

Procedure for Implementing IEPC

Step One: Choose a tradebook, basal selection, or content area passage with good potential for developing imagery.

Step Two: Display the IEPC blank form on the overhead projector or on a large chart paper. Tell students they will use their imaginations to create pictures in their minds about what they'll be reading. Tell them that creating pictures before, during and after reading helps them comprehend and remember what they read.

Step Three: Using the blank IEPC form, explain the four components of the IEPC.

Prereading Stage

Step Four: Tell students to close their eyes and imagine everything they can about the text to be read or video to be watched. This can be based on the book's cover, title, or topic. Remind students to use their senses . . . feelings, taste, smell, sight, surroundings . . . as they imagine.

Step Five: Talk about their mental images with their partners and ask the class to add anything else that comes to mind. Write their responses in the "I" column on the form.

Step Six: Show the students how to use their visual images and add details, prior experiences, anecdotes, other sensory information, and so forth. Write this information in the "E" column on the form.

Step Seven: Talk about at least one sample prediction, based upon earlier visual images. Encourage the students to do the same, and write their responses in the "P" column.

Reading Stage

Step Eight: Here, students will read or listen to the text, or watch the video with their predictions in mind.

Postreading Stage

Step Nine: After reading/listening/viewing, go back to the transparency and, with a different colored marker, adjust the original predictions to go along with the newly learned information.

BLANK IEPC FORM

I	E	P	C
Close your eyes and imagine the scene, character, events, setting, problem. What do you see, feel, hear, smell? Share your thinking with a partner.	Elaborate—tell/describe/ give details of what you "see" in your mind.	Use these ideas to make some predictions/guesses about the passages to be read/listened to, or video to be viewed.	Read/Listen to/View to confirm or change your predictions about the text.

Types of Propaganda Techniques (Critical Reading and Viewing)

One aspect of critical reading that readers must understand and learn to recognize is **propaganda.** Propaganda is a systematic dissemination or promotion of particular ideas, doctrines, or practices to further one's own cause or to damage an opposing one through the use of words and nonverbal symbols. In short, it is an "attempt to persuade others to accept certain beliefs or opinions" (Gunning, 2000, 284). Elementary children not only encounter propaganda techniques in written texts they read, but they are also bombarded with propaganda every day through television and electronic media. When readers learn, through careful, thoughtful instruction, that the purpose of propaganda is to sway their judgment and opinion, they become better critical readers and are more equipped to make informed judgments based on the facts as opposed to emotional appeals that propaganda techniques use. There are many types of propaganda techniques; however, the following are most frequently taught in schools.

1. **Testimonial**
   "Well-known personalities testify or speak out for an idea or product. This technique is frequently used in advertisements in which a sports star endorses a shampoo or a TV star urges consumers to buy a certain brand of toothpaste." [Most widely used, easiest to understand—Start with testimonial]

2. **Bandwagon**
   "Playing on the natural desire to be part of the crowd, this technique tries to convince by stating that because so many others are buying a product or taking certain action, we should too."

3. **Card Stacking**
   "This method lists all the good points or advantages of an idea or product but none of its bad points or disadvantages."

4. **Plain Folks**
   "To win our trust, a person of power or wealth tries to convince us that she or he is an ordinary person just like us."

5. **Name Calling**
   "Words that may have unfavorable connotations such as *nerd, tightwad, liberal,* or *spendthrift* are used to describe opposing political candidates, competing products, or rival ideas." We respond emotionally to the name, thus failing to consider the people, products, or ideas in a rational manner.

6. **Glittering Generalities**
   "The near opposite of name calling, glittering generalities are favorable-sounding abstract terms or scientific words that usually evoke a positive response. Examples are *justice, honesty, new, miracle ingredients,* and scientific-sounding names like *benzoyl peroxide.*"

7. **Transfer**
   "In this device, the favorable feeling we have for a symbol, person, or object is carried over or transferred to an idea or product someone is trying to sell." Example: "A candidate for political office is seen standing next to a flag with her family, which includes a big, friendly collie." The positive feelings we have are transferred to the candidate. (pp. 284–285)

From: *Creating Literacy for All Children* by T.G. Gunning.

Problem-Solution Chart

What is the problem?	
Whose problem is it? Why is it a problem?	
What are three possible solutions?	**Pros and Cons for each solution**
1.	(+) (−)
2.	(+) (−)
3.	(+) (−)
What is the best solution and why?	

Adapted by: Alice F. Snyder, 2000, from course materials, I&L 2212, Methods and Materials in Teaching Reading, University of Pittsburgh, Pittsburgh, PA, 1995.

Compare-Contrast Chart

Major Topic/Idea/Event	What is being compared or contrasted?	Major Topic/Idea/Event

Example:

Woodland Tribes	Aspects of their Culture	Plains Tribes
	Methods of transportation	
	What they ate	
	Their clothing	
	Their houses	
	Geography of the region where they lived	
	Their customs	
	Status of women in tribe	

Adapted from: Norton, T. & Jackson Land, B.L. (2008). *50 literacy strategies for beginning teachers, 1–8.* (2nd ed.). Upper Saddle River, NJ: Merrill/Prentice Hall (p. 112).

Chapter Two

Strategies for
Vocabulary Development

Word Knowledge Rating Scale

A great *before reading* informal assessment device, the word knowledge rating scale (WKRS) is used to determine a child's or group of children's prior knowledge of vocabulary that they will encounter in a text that will be read. Using *Dale's Stages of Word Knowledge* (1965), the teacher selects various words from the upcoming text, and places them down the left side of a table that is labeled with three of the stages of word knowledge (know it well, have seen or heard it, and unknown/no clue). The student checks the appropriate column for each word, depending on the level of word knowledge he/she has for each word listed. A fourth column is recommended, in which students write a short definition in their own words for the words they check as knowing very well, so the teacher can determine if the student does, indeed, have an understanding of the word as it is used in the text to be read. The WKRS is not graded.

Word Knowledge Rating Scale

[Steig, W. (1971). *Amos and Boris.* New York: Farrar Straus and Giroux.]

Word	Know It well	Have seen or heard it	No clue!	If know it well, write a short definition in your own words
breakers				
backwashes				
navigation				
sextant				
compass				
telescope				
enterprise				
luminous				
phosphorescent				
sound/sounded				
daintiness				
plankton				
mote				
admiration				
evaded				
abounding				
radiance				
incidence				
desperate				
privilege				

Adapted from: Blachowicz, C. (1986). Making connections: Alternatives to the vocabulary notebook, *Journal of Reading,* 29(7), 643–649.

Word Knowledge Rating Scale for Grades 1–2

[Words from: Ehlert, L. (2001). *Waiting for wings.* San Diego, CA: Harcourt, Inc.]

Directions: Use the happy faces to tell how well you know these words. This isn't a test and you won't be graded. Remember: You aren't supposed to know all the words.

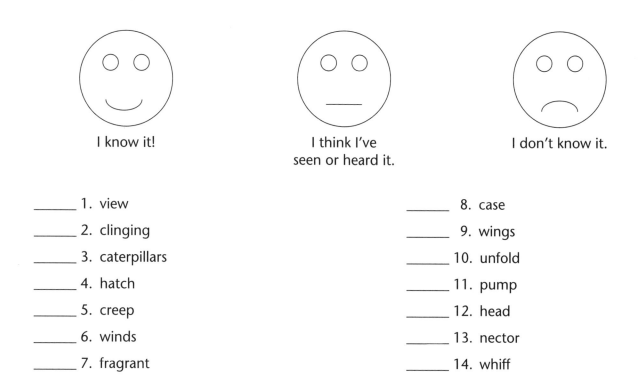

I know it!

I think I've seen or heard it.

I don't know it.

_____ 1. view

_____ 2. clinging

_____ 3. caterpillars

_____ 4. hatch

_____ 5. creep

_____ 6. winds

_____ 7. fragrant

_____ 8. case

_____ 9. wings

_____ 10. unfold

_____ 11. pump

_____ 12. head

_____ 13. nector

_____ 14. whiff

For the words you know, in the space below, write a meaning for each word in your own words.

CSSR Flow Chart Strategy for "What to Do When You Come to a Word You Don't Know"

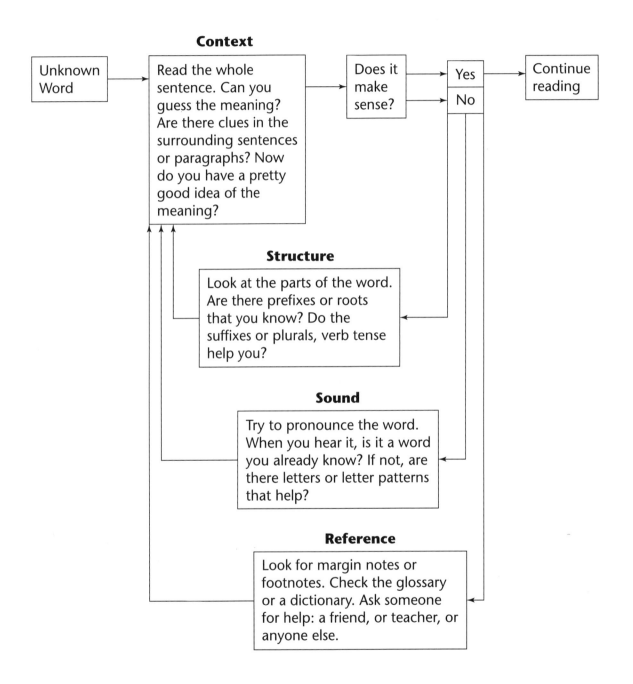

Context

Unknown Word → Read the whole sentence. Can you guess the meaning? Are there clues in the surrounding sentences or paragraphs? Now do you have a pretty good idea of the meaning? → Does it make sense? → Yes / No → Continue reading

Structure

Look at the parts of the word. Are there prefixes or roots that you know? Do the suffixes or plurals, verb tense help you?

Sound

Try to pronounce the word. When you hear it, is it a word you already know? If not, are there letters or letter patterns that help?

Reference

Look for margin notes or footnotes. Check the glossary or a dictionary. Ask someone for help: a friend, or teacher, or anyone else.

From *Teaching Content Reading and Writing* by M.R. Ruddell. Reprinted by permission of John Wiley & Sons, Inc.

Classification

Directions: Read the list of words below. Think about how the words are similar and belong together. Write a word or phrase on the line that identifies what the words have in common.

bear   ocean liner

cat   airplane

whale   motorcycle

lion   automobile

horse   train

mouse   bus

_____   _____

Classification with the Intruder

Directions: Read the list of words below. All of the words in the list have something in common except one. On the line below, write the word or phrase that identifies what category or concept describes the words. Then circle the Intruder (word that doesn't belong).

punt   duck

pass   pigeon

receive   robin

dribble   eagle

run   chicken

block   salamander

tackle   seagull

_____   _____

Pictorial Word Webs/Maps

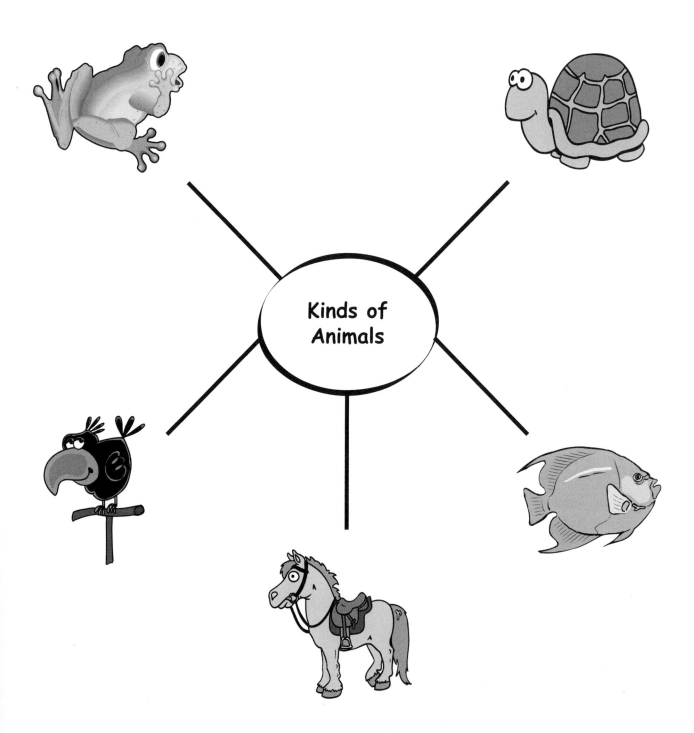

Kinds of
Animals

Semantic Word Map

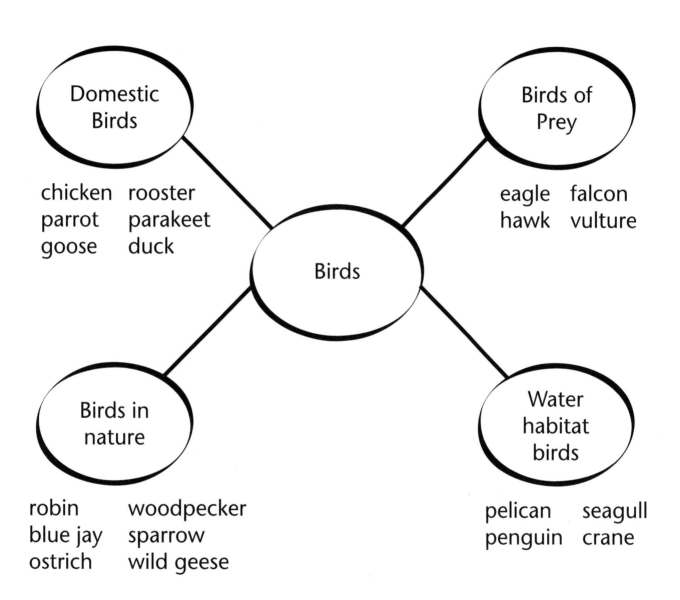

Domestic Birds

chicken rooster
parrot parakeet
goose duck

Birds of Prey

eagle falcon
hawk vulture

Birds

Birds in nature

robin woodpecker
blue jay sparrow
ostrich wild geese

Water habitat birds

pelican seagull
penguin crane

Created by Alice Snyder. Semantic Webs by W. Nagy, adapted from Johnson and Pearson, 1984.

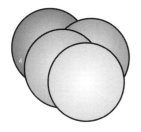
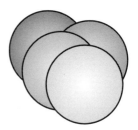

Concept Circles

Concept Circles is an excellent instructional strategy for teaching vocabulary by relating words that exemplify a concept or category. Similar conceptually to categorization, students are required to determine how the words in the circle are related and then identify the concept or category depicted by the words in the circle. There are three different tasks that can be created with concept circles. The task directions must be included with each concept circle as well as a blank on which the child writes the concept.

The three tasks are:

1. What do all the words in the circle have in common? Write the concept or category on the line.

2. Shade in the section that contains a word that doesn't belong. Then identify what the other words have in common. Write the concept or category on the line.

3. What do all the words in the circle have in common? Write another word that goes with that concept/category. Write the concept/category on the line.

Hint: To create concept circles, it is easier first to think about the concept or category you want the students to identify, then determine words that exemplify or are examples of that concept or category. Concept circles are not used to identify character traits or actions of characters or historical people and subsequently ask the students to identify the character or historical figure. People/characters in a book or movie are not concepts. See examples on the next few pages.

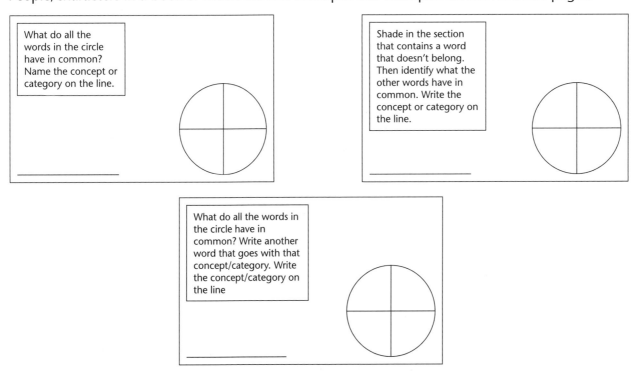

What do all the words in the circle have in common? Name the concept or category on the line.

Shade in the section that contains a word that doesn't belong. Then identify what the other words have in common. Write the concept or category on the line.

What do all the words in the circle have in common? Write another word that goes with that concept/category. Write the concept/category on the line

---

From: Vacca, R.T. & Vacca, J.L. (1996). *Content area reading* (5th Ed.). New York: Harper Collins.

Example of Concept Circles

Tasks 1 and 2

Directions:
What do all of the words in the circle have in common? Write the category/concept on the line.

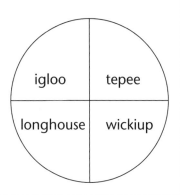

_____

Directions:
Shade in the section that contains a word that doesn't belong. Then identify what the other words have in common. Write the concept/category on the line.

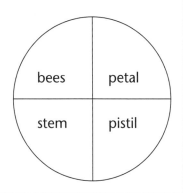

_____

Concept of Definition Map

The Concept of Definition Map (CD Map) provides an organizational framework for learning conceptual information about vocabulary words that represent concepts. Three types of relationships are explored about a word using the CD Map. The first, categories, is explored by asking "What is it?" Students determine what category the term represents. The second relationship is properties, which is examined by asking "What is it like?" Students list three characteristics of the concept. The third relationship is illustrations, which is explored by asking "What are some examples?" Students list three concrete examples of the concept. Another feature of the CD Map is added by having students identify an example to compare the conceptual term or an example of an opposite of the term, in other words, "What is not an example of the concept?" or "What is the opposite of this concept?" See the blank example below:

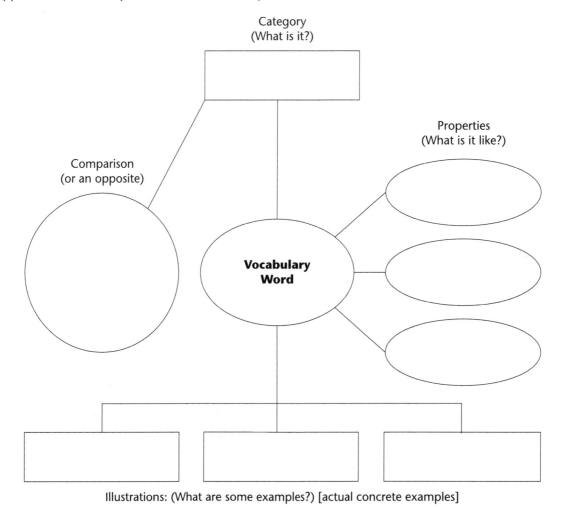

Illustrations: (What are some examples?) [actual concrete examples]

From Schwartz, R.M. (1988). Learning to learn vocabulary in content area textbooks. *Journal of Reading, 32,* 108–118.

Example Concept of Definition Map

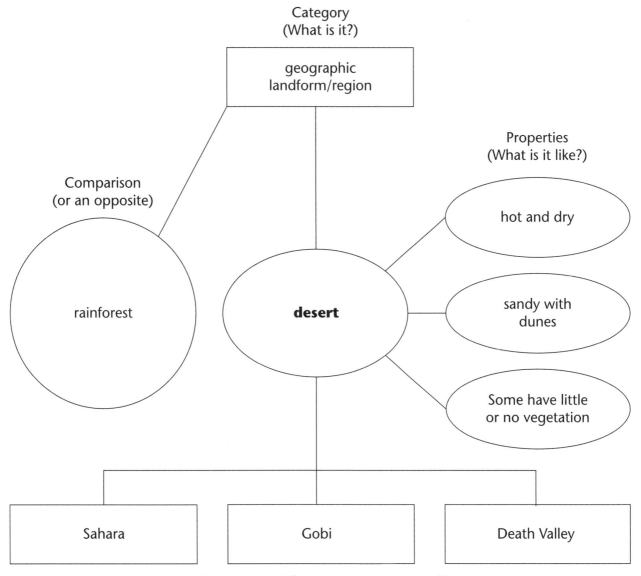

Category
(What is it?)

geographic
landform/region

Comparison
(or an opposite)

Properties
(What is it like?)

rainforest

desert

hot and dry

sandy with
dunes

Some have little
or no vegetation

Sahara

Gobi

Death Valley

Illustrations: (What are some examples?)

Adapted from Schwartz, R.M. (1988). Learning to learn vocabulary in content area textbooks. *Journal of Reading, 32,* 108–118.

Snyder Word Analysis Map (SWAM)

I developed the **Snyder Word Analysis Map (SWAM)** in 1998 to help my college developmental reading students establish a more in-depth understanding of vocabulary words by exploring various semantic aspects of the word using a dictionary and/or thesaurus. According to Beck, McKeown, and Omanson (1987), students need multiple exposures to new words in order to learn their meanings at an in-depth level. Therefore, I utilized as many different ways I could to help my students learn new vocabulary. One of those methods was Schwartz's Concept of Definition Map (1988). I liked the design of this map and saw my students' success with learning conceptual terms using the Concept of Definition Map, but realized that this graphic organizer did not work as well with all words, especially those that did not concretely represent concepts. Therefore, I developed the SWAM, using a modified design of the Schwartz map. I also used the SWAM as one of several ways to expose my fourth graders to learning vocabulary in all subject areas and they successfully learned the words at a more in-depth level as a result of completing the SWAM.

First, students are asked to write a short dictionary definition, then analyze the word by determining how many syllables it has, what part of speech it is, based on how the word is used in the text from which it came, if it contains any prefixes and/or suffixes and if so, what their meanings are, whether the word has a root and if so, what its origin and meaning is. The student is also asked to provide three synonyms for the word in the same part of speech as the target word, one antonym in the same part of speech, and finally, to write a sentence using the word with good context clues.

I teach my students to create a "skeleton" map of the SWAM by having them think of it like a clock. They begin at the middle where they write the target word. Then at 12:00, they write a short definition. At 2:00, 3:00, 4:00, they write the analysis of the word as indicated above. At 5:00, 6:00, and 7:00, they write three synonyms. At 9:00 they write an antonym, and at 11:00, they write their context clues sentence. After completing the SWAM, a student comes away with a more in-depth understanding of the word and is able to formulate a good definition along with an example sentence. An additional task that can be included to the SWAM is an illustration of the word, either drawn by the student or cut and pasted to the page. Students can develop a SWAM based on a given vocabulary word and then, after the teacher checks his or her work, the student can teach the assigned word to the class after converting his/her map to an overhead transparency. By presenting the SWAM, the student's knowledge of the word is developed even further. See the examples on the following pages.

Beck, I.L., McKeown, M.G., & Omanson, R.C. (1987). The effects and uses of diverse vocabulary instructional techniques. In M.G. McKeown & M.E. Curtis (Eds.). *The nature of vocabulary acquisition* (pp. 147–163). Hillsdale, NJ: Erlbaum.

Schwartz, R. (1988). Learning to learn vocabulary in content area textbooks. *Journal of Reading, 32,* 108–118.

Snyder Word Analysis Map (SWAM)

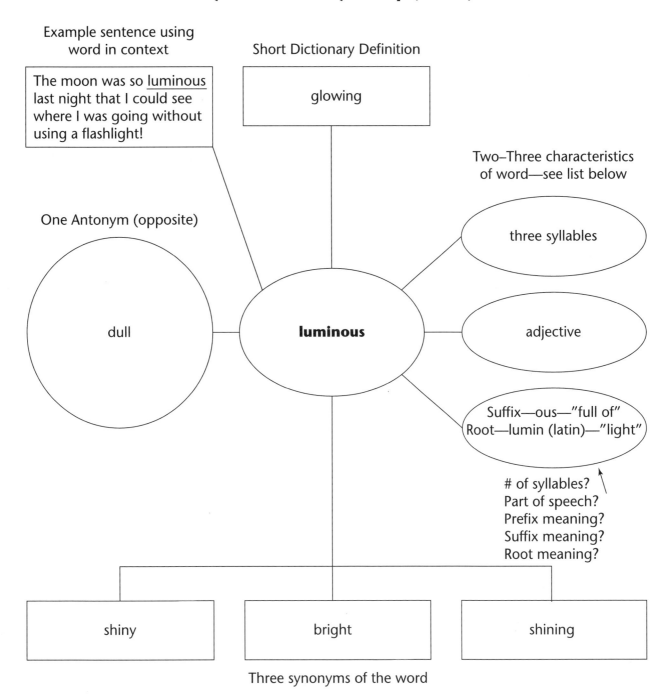

Example sentence using word in context

The moon was so <u>luminous</u> last night that I could see where I was going without using a flashlight!

Short Dictionary Definition

glowing

Two–Three characteristics of word—see list below

three syllables

One Antonym (opposite)

dull

luminous

adjective

Suffix—ous—"full of"
Root—lumin (latin)—"light"

# of syllables?
Part of speech?
Prefix meaning?
Suffix meaning?
Root meaning?

shiny

bright

shining

Three synonyms of the word

Example created by Alice F. Snyder, 2004.

Snyder Word Analysis Map (SWAM), adapted from Schwartz

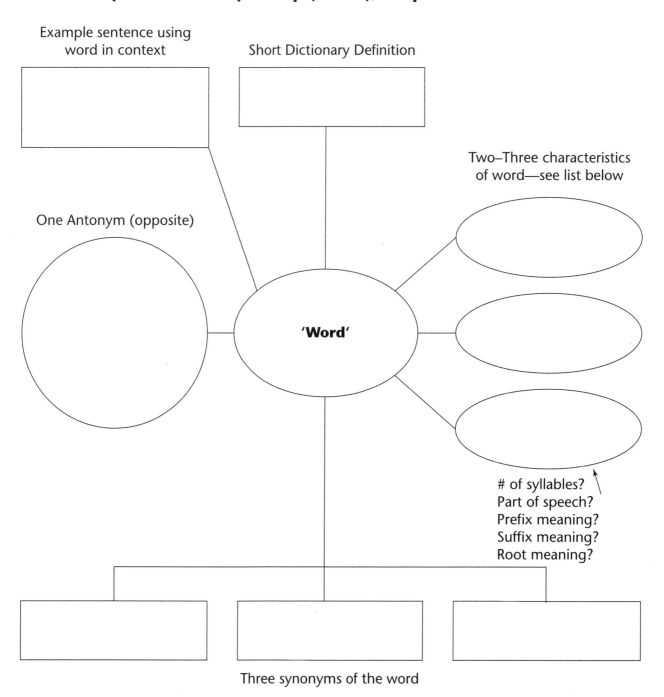

Example sentence using
word in context

Short Dictionary Definition

Two–Three characteristics
of word—see list below

One Antonym (opposite)

'Word'

# of syllables?
Part of speech?
Prefix meaning?
Suffix meaning?
Root meaning?

Three synonyms of the word

Design of graphic organizer adapted by Alice F. Snyder, 1998, from Robert Schwartz Concept of Definition Map, 1988.

Vocabulary Venn Diagram

Some very simple words in our language have more than one meaning. A vocabulary Venn Diagram is a useful and simple way to show children these multiple meaning words. Place the word that has at least two meanings in the intersected area of the Venn Diagram. Have children determine other meanings of the word and place them in the circle areas that have not been intersected. Use one word or short phrases as references to the meanings.

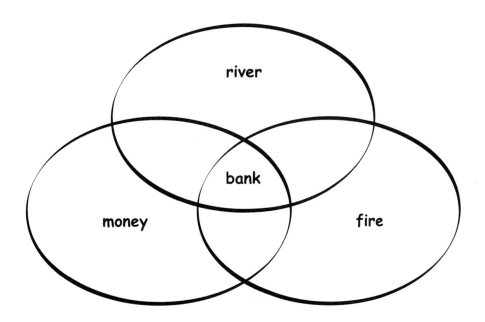

Word Clusters

Another strategy that works well with words that have more than one meaning is **Word Clusters.** The student writes a word that has two or more meanings at the top center of a sheet of construction paper or large index card. Using a dictionary, the student researches different meanings of the word. Drawing lines from the vocabulary word, the student writes a short definition at the end of each line and then draws a picture to illustrate that meaning. The part of speech, a short sentence composed by the student, and/or the word's origin (etymology) can also be added for each different meaning to further enhance the student's understanding of the word. See the next page for a list of words that have **more than five (5)** meanings.

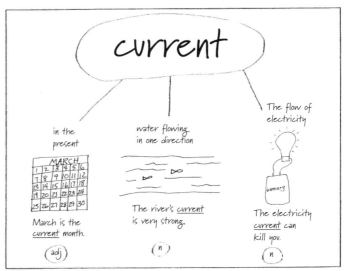

Seventh grader's Word Cluster for 10 meanings of 'Hot'

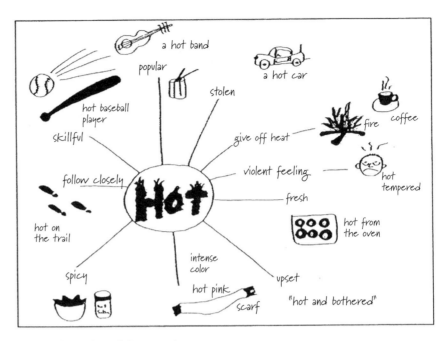

Common words that have more than five (5) meanings:

act	air	around	away	bad	bank
bar	base	black	blow	boat	break
by	carry	case	cast	catch	change
charge	check	clear	close	color	count
court	cover	crack	cross	crown	cut
dead	deep	draw	dress	drive	dry
dull	even	eye	face	fail	fair
fall	fast	fight	fire	fly	good
green	hand	head	have	heel	high
hold	horn	hot	house	in	just
keep	key	knock	know	lay	leave
line	low	make	man	mark	measure
mind	mine	natural	new	no	nose
note	now	number	of	off	on
open	out	over	paper	part	pass
pay	pick	picture	piece	pipe	pitch
place	plain	plant	plate	play	point
positive	post	power	print	put	quiet
rain	raise	range	reach	rear	rest
return	rich	ride	right	ring	rise
roll	round	rule	run	scale	score
send	serve	set	sharp	shift	shine
shoot	short	shot	show	side	sight
sign	sing	sink	sit	slip	small
snap	so	sound	spin	spread	spring
square	stamp	star	start	stay	step
stick	stiff	stock	stop	strike	stroke
strong	stuff	sweep	sweet	swing	switch
tack	take	thick	thing	think	through
throw	tic	tight	time	to	touch
tough	train	trip	turn	twist	under
up	use	warm	watch	way	wear

Name: _____

Vocabulary Star

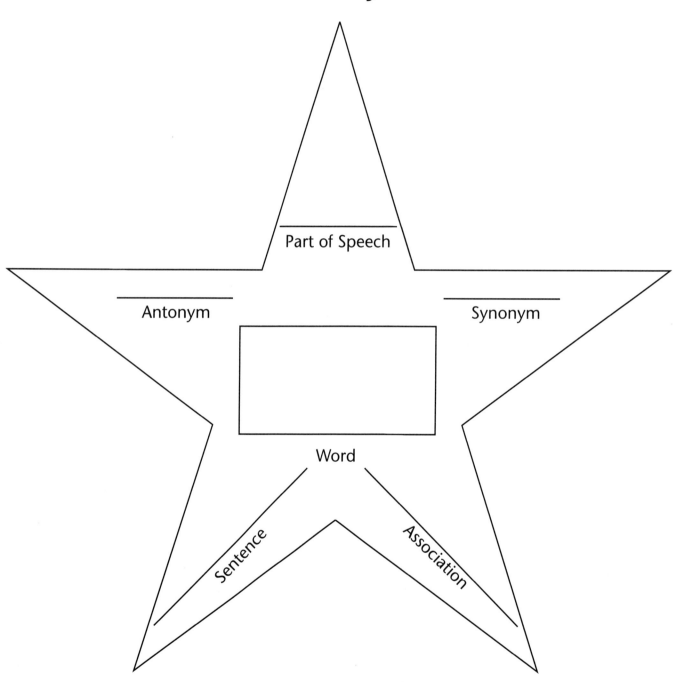

Part of Speech

Antonym

Synonym

Word

Sentence

Association

Reprinted by Alice Snyder, from workshop materials, 50th Annual College Reading Association Conference, 2006.

Semantic Feature Analysis (Word Matrix)

The Semantic Feature Analysis or Word Matrix (P. Anders & C. Bos, 1986) is a useful graphic organizer for vocabulary development that helps students see the relationships among concepts and terms that may be found within a single text or between multiple texts before, during, and after reading about a particular topic. Place the given vocabulary words down the left side of the matrix. Across the top, list specific features that the terms may or may not have in common. Then provide a code for how students should mark the boxes for each word when determining whether the word does or does not contain or demonstrate the feature.

	Historical	Modern	Made of metal	Protects someone	Hurts someone	A type of person	Something soldiers wear
armor	+	–	+	+	–	–	+
shield	+	–	+	+	–	–	–
weapon	+	+	+	?	+	–	–
sword	+	–	+	?	+	–	?
helmet	+	+	+	+	–	–	+
cross-bow	+	–	?	?	+	–	–
warrior	+	?	–	+	+	+	–
army	+	+	–	+	+	+	–
tunic	+	–	–	–	–	–	+
champion	+	+	–	+	+	+	–
bearers	+	–	–	–	–	+	–

Key: + if yes
      – if no
      ? if not sure

Semantic Feature Analysis (Word Matrix)

The Solar System

	Is an inner planet	Is an outer planet	Has an atmo-sphere	Supports life	Made of rock and metal	Made of gas	Has moons	Has rings
Mercury	√	O	O	O	√	O	O	O
Venus	√	O	√	O	√	O	O	O
Earth	?	?	√	√	√	O	√	O
Mars	O	√	√	O	√	O	√	O
Jupiter	O	√	O	O	O	√	√	√
Saturn	O	√	O	O	√	O	√	√
Uranus	O	√	O	O	√	O	√	√
Neptune	O	√	O	O	√	O	√	O

Key: √ **if yes**
O **if no**
? **if not sure**

From Tompkins, Gail E. *Literacy for the 21st Century: Teaching Reading and Writing in Grades 4 through 8,* 1/e Published by Allyn and Bacon/Merrill Education, Boston, MA. Copyright © 2004 by Pearson Education. Reprinted by permission of the publisher.

Vocabulary Illustrations/
Vocabulary Pictures

Developed by Joe Antinarella (Tidewater Community College, Chesapeake, Virginia)

A helpful way to provide opportunities for students to demonstrate word knowledge is with Vocabulary Illustrations/Vocabulary Pictures. Using this strategy allows students to draw what they understand about word meanings. Students choose or are given a word and write the word and its definition on a piece of drawing paper. The student finds a picture or draws a picture that illustrates the concept or word. Below the picture, the student writes a sentence that clarifies or goes along with what is happening in the picture or drawing. A short definition can also be added. Below are examples:

Goalie

A goal keeper

by Michael

If I played soccer I would be a goalie.

Opulence

Definition: excessive wealth, grandeur

These four pictures are a good example of opulence because those things are things people with excessive wealth could afford to have.

The sun has light and is warm.

The sun has light and is warm.

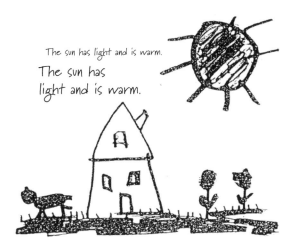

From Richardson/Morgan/Fleener. *Reading to Learn in the Content Areas* (with CD-ROM and InfoTrac®), 6E. © Wadsworth, a part of Cengage Learning, Inc. Reproduced by permission. www.cengage.com/permissions.

Vocabulary Pictures

Students find and glue a picture to depict their understanding of the meaning of given vocabulary words. Students write the word at the top and a short definition for the word. Below the picture, the student writes a sentence that goes along with what's happening in the picture or drawing. For example . . .

mast

a tall pole that holds up the sail on a sailboat

Mast

The strong wind bent the mast
that held up the sails!

mansion

a very large house with many
rooms where rich people live

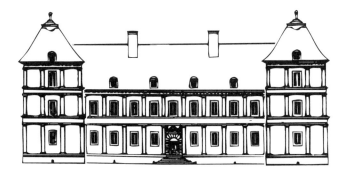

Bill Gates lives in a mansion
because he is very rich.

Homophone Picture Cards

(Can be collected and made into a class book)

hare

The <u>hare</u> likes carrots.

hair

I have long, brown <u>hair</u>.

fowl

The bird is a water <u>fowl</u>.

foul

The batter hit a <u>foul</u> ball.

Homophone Picture Cards developed by Kelli Lawson and Cari Viramontes.

Examples created by A. Snyder.

List of Homophones
(Words that sound alike but are spelled differently)

air-heir	coarse-course	hoard-horde	pair-pear-pare	serf-surf
allowed-aloud	colonel-kernel	hoarse-horse	palette-pallet	sew-so-sow
ant-aunt	complement-	hoes-hose	passed-past	shear-sheer
ate-eight	compliment	hole-whole	patience-patients	shone-shown
ball-bawl	council-counsel	hour-our	pause-paws	shoot-chute
band-banned	creak-creek	jam-jamb	peace-piece	side-sighed
bare-bear	days-daze	knead-need	peak-peek-pique	sighs-size
base-bass	dear-deer	knew-new	peal-peel	slay-sleigh
based-baste	dense-dents	knight-night	pedal-peddle	soar-sore
be-bee	dew-do-due	knot-not	peer-pier	soared-sword
beat-beet	die-dye	know-no	phase-faze	sole-soul
bell-belle	doe-dough	lacks-lax	plain-plane	some-sum
berry-bury	dual-duel	lead-led	plait-plate	son-sun
berth-birth	ewe-you	leak-leek	pleas-please	stairs-stares
billed-build	eye-I	leased-least	pole-poll	stake-steak
blew-blue	fair-fare	lie-lye	pore-pour	stationary-
boar-bore	feat-feet	links-lynx	praise-prays-preys	stationery
board-bored	fined-find	load-lode	presence-presents	steal-steel
boarder-border	fir-fur	loan-lone	pride-pried	straight-strait
born-borne	flea-flee	loot-lute	prince-prints	suite-sweet
bough-bow	flew-flu	made-maid	principal-principle	tail-tale
brake-break	floe-flow	mail-male	profit-prophet	taught-taut
bread-bred	flour-flower	main-mane	quarts-quartz	tear-tier
brews-bruise	foaled-fold	maize-maze	rain-rein-reign	tense-tents
bridal-bridle	for-fore-four	manner-manor	raise-rays-raze	their-they're-there
brows-browse	forth-fourth	marshal-martial	rap-wrap	threw-through
buy-by-bye	foul-fowl	meat-meet-mete	real-reel	throne-thrown
cache-cash	gait-gate	medal-meddle-	red-read	tide-tied
callous-callus	genes-jeans	metal	reed-read	to-too-two
capital-capitol	gofer-gopher	might-mite	rest-wrest	toad-toed-towed
carat-carrot	gorilla-guerilla	mind-mined	right-rite-write	toe-tow
cast-caste	grate-great	miner-minor	ring-wring	tracked-tract
cede-seed	grill-grille	missed-mist	road-rode-rowed	troop-troupe
ceiling-sealing	groan-grown	moan-mown	role-roll	undo-undue
cell-sell	guessed-guest	moose-mousse	roomer-rumor	vain-vane-vein
cellar-seller	hail-hale	morning-mourning	root-route	wade-weighed
cent-scent-sent	hair-hare	muscle-mussel	rose-rows	waist-waste
chews-choose	hall-haul	naval-navel	rote-wrote	wait-weight
chic-sheik	halve-have	none-nun	rung-wrung	waive-wave
chili-chilly	hangar-hanger	oar-or-ore	sac-sack	wares-wears
choral-coral	hay-hey	one-won	sail-sale	warn-worn
chord-cord-cored	heal-heel	paced-paste	scene-seen	way-weigh
chute-shoot	hear-here	packed-pact	sea-see	weak-week
cite-sight-site	heard-herd	pail-pale	sealing-ceiling	wood-would
clause-claws	heroin-heroine	pain-pane	seam-seem	yoke-yolk
close-clothes	hi-high			

Word Splash

Example of a word splash with content vocabulary for *Owen and Mzee: The True Story of a Remarkable Friendship*, by Isabella Hatkoff, Craig Hatkoff, and Dr. Paula Kahumbu (2006, New York, Scholastic).

tortoise   mud wallow   companion

coral reef   ecologist

commotion   animal sanctuary   pod

caretaker   *Swahili*   **enclosure**

bushbacks   **hippopotamus**

protective presence   resilence

Word Splash:
A variety of words (5–15, depending on grade level) are written randomly across a paper (transparency) or chalkboard. If typed on a handout, it is useful to use a variety of text fonts and sizes. Most words are unknown vocabulary words, but a few might be more common words that will give clues about the content, characters, or setting (depending on what genre of book the words are taken from). A student chooses any word from the set and then gives a sentence or definition. The teacher expands with an example, steering the discussion to its usage in the text. The process continues until all words are discussed. Then the students are asked to predict the story or text information based on the words.

Semantic Impressions

Semantic Impressions is a strategy that incorporates students' prediction skills and prior word knowledge as they create a story using vocabulary words and phrases from a book they will be reading. **The teacher chooses and lists between 5 and 20 key words** that are central to the plot of a narrative story or chapter book in the order they appear in the story (either on overhead, chalkboard, or chart paper). The teacher briefly goes over the meanings of each word, encouraging student input, then discusses the three rules of the activity: 1. Words/phrases must be used in order they appear on the list. 2. Once a word is used, it can be reused. 3. The form of words (plurals, tenses, parts of speech) can be changed. **As a group, students will compose** a sensible story based on the words. The story should have a beginning, middle, and end (or problem and resolution). Students may compose a written story, or it may be done as a class orally. As students give their oral contributions, the **teacher writes their Semantic Impressions story on the board, overhead, or chart paper**, helping students to formulate a cohesive narrative with a sensible flow. Students' sentences can be combined. When story is finished, the teacher has the class edit it, then read, or listen to, the published narrative.

Example: Words from book *Amos and Boris* (William Steig, 1971)

1. mouse
2. bursting breakers
3. navigation
4. necessities
5. boat
6. phosphorescent
7. luminous water
8. treading water
9. vast loneliness
10. mammal
11. whale
12. Ivory Coast
13. sounded
14. plankton
15. tidal wave
16. breaded with sand

Sample Story Impression (Created by Noelle Snyder, 1992):

A Scary Day at Sea

Once there was a **mouse** named Amos. He was going to sail on the ocean to visit his mouse cousins far away. When he was getting ready for the trip, he saw **bursting breakers** in the fuse box in the basement of his house. He had to fix the breakers and that delayed his trip. Soon he learned everything about **navigation**, so he loaded his **boat** with all the **necessities** he would need. He started out the next day. Soon he couldn't see the **phosphorescent** lights on land, but the moon was out and the **luminous water** was pretty. But he felt alone in the **vast loneliness** of the ocean! Feeling lonesome and bored, he began to wonder what he, a tiny **mammal**, was doing out on the middle of the big ocean! All of a sudden, a **whale** named Boris came up from under the water and scared the daylights out of Amos! Amos was so scared, he almost fell off the boat! Boris introduced himself and told Amos he was sorry for scaring him. Amos asked if Boris would show him the way to the **Ivory Coast**, where he was going to visit his cousins. Boris said "Of course! I would be happy to!" Then Boris made this loud **sound** that scared Amos again! "What was that noise?" asked Amos. Boris told him that he saw a lot of **plankton** in the water and that was good food to eat! They both ate a lot of plankton until they were full. Soon a big **tidal wave** came and washed Boris and Amos up on shore of the Ivory Coast. Boris was in trouble. He couldn't get back in the water because the wave pushed him far up on the beach. Fortunately for Boris, Amos had lots of friends there. He went off to find them and they quickly came and helped push him back in the water. He was **breaded with sand**, but once he got into the water, he washed himself off. Boris was very grateful to Amos for saving his life.

Margaret Ann Richek, in *The Reading Teacher*, 2005, vol. 58, no. 5, pp. 414–423 (originally called *Story Impressions* by McGinley & Denner, 1987).

Vocab-o-Gram (Predict-o-Gram)	
Use vocabulary list provided to make predictions about . . .	
The setting	What will the setting be like?
The characters	Any ideas about the characters?
The problem or goal	What might it be?
The actions	What might happen?
The resolution	How might it end?
What question(s) do you have?	
Mystery words:	

Word List:

From: Blachowicz, C.L.Z. (1986). "Making connections: Alternatives to the vocabulary notebook," *Journal of Reading, 29*, 643–649.

Vocab-o-Gram (Predict-o-Gram)

Use vocabulary list provided to make predictions about . . .

The setting beach sea boat Ivory Coast	What will the setting be like? It takes place on a beach by the sea in a place called the Ivory Coast
The characters mouse mammal whale elephants	Any ideas about the characters? There's a mouse, a whale and elephants. They are all mammals.
The problem or goal hurricane tidal wave	What might it be? A hurricane hits their beach that makes a big tidal wave that comes.
The actions boat breakers drown sound	What might happen? The tidal wave makes big breakers that tip over a boat and makes the mouse drown.
The resolution boat The Rodent	How might it end? A rodent gets a boat to resku the mouse or maybe the whale helps.
What question(s) do you have? What is navigation?	
Mystery words: plankton luminous compass	

Word List:

sound	breakers	navigation	luminous	plankton	mouse
sea	hurricane	beach	elephants	mammal	boat
drown	compass	tidal wave	The Rodent	whale	Ivory Coast

Blachowicz, C.L.Z. (1986). "Making connections: Alternatives to the vocabulary notebook," *Journal of Reading, 29,* 643–649.

Word Expert Cards

Word Expert Cards is another strategy that allows children to combine drawing with various aspects of vocabulary learning from fiction and non-fiction texts. The teacher identifies a list of 50–100 key words from a chapter book or unit of study, for example, using a combination of the content area textbook and various non-fiction and electronic texts. Each student receives 2–4 words for which to develop Word Expert Cards. The teacher writes a page number beside each word so the students can find the words in the indicated text. Students are given sheets of construction paper or large index cards to create a Word Expert Card for each word. **Directions** are given to students as follows:

1. Use the page number to locate the word in the text.
2. **<u>Copy the sentence containing the word</u>** inside the card.
3. Use a dictionary to look up the definition for each word; Discuss it with others.
4. On scratch paper, write the **<u>part of speech</u>** and the **<u>definition in your own words</u>** that matches the use of the word in the story.
5. Then, on the scratch paper, **<u>write your own sentence using the word</u>**.
6. Get the definition and sentence approved for accuracy by the teacher.
7. Copy onto the inside of your card the **approved** definition, part of speech, and sentence.
8. Write the vocabulary word on the front outside of the card in big bold letters.
9. On the front of the card, **<u>illustrate the vocabulary word</u>** neatly and creatively. Get your illustration approved.
10. Write your name and word on the back side of the card.

Examples:

igneous—p. 6	blunderbuss—p. 4
• **Sentence where found**—The names describe how the rocks were made—sedimentary means "made from sediment," **igneous** means "fiery," and metamorphic means "changed." • **Part of speech**—adjective • **Definition**—produced by the action of fire; formed by volcanic action or intense heat, as rocks solidified from molten magma at or below the surface of the earth • **My own sentence**—We saw lots of igneous rocks when we went exploring near the volcanoes in Hawaii.	• **Sentence where found**—"I'll take your old blunderbuss with me," his father had said. • **Part of speech**—noun • **Definition**—an obsolete short gun with a large bore and a broad, flaring muzzle, accurate only at close range • **My own sentence**—The pilgrim had only a blunderbuss gun to use to hunt for turkey and deer, so he wasn't able to bring back much food for the family. 

From: Margaret Ann Richek in *The Reading Teacher,* 2005, vol. 58, no. 5, pp. 414–423 (originally by Landsdown 1991).

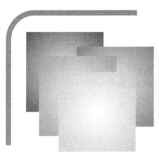

Magic Squares

Magic Squares is an instructional strategy that can be used at all levels, with content vocabulary and vocabulary found in children's literature. The Magic Square is a special arrangement of numbers that when added across, down, or diagonally always equals the same sum. Students match a series of definitions or word explanations (labeled with numbers) to the vocabulary placed in the squares. Students write the number of the definition that matches the word in the square. If their answers are correct, the sum of the numbers when added across, down, or diagonally will be the same. **See directions on next page for how to make magic square combinations.**

Some possible Magic Square combinations:

8	1	6
3	5	7
4	9	2

15

6	7	2
1	5	9
8	3	4

15

9	2	7
4	6	8
5	10	3

18

5	4	9
10	6	2
3	8	7

18

16	2	3	13
5	11	10	8
9	7	6	12
4	14	15	1

34

14	9	5	16
14	7	11	2
15	6	10	3
1	12	8	13

34

Example of elementary grade Magic Square on the Ancient World
Developed by Ed Toscano

Directions: Read each of the sentences below the magic square. Match the sentence to the correct word on the square. Put the number of the sentence in that box. If your answers are correct, the sum of the numbers when added across or down (or diagonally) will be the same.

Parthenon _____	Olympics _____	Slaves _____
Athens _____	Columns _____	Arches _____
Republic _____	Aqueduct _____	Rome _____

1. The sporting event the Greeks invented to help train warriors.
2. This city ruled the largest empire in the world.
3. This city was the largest direct democracy in the world.
4. The type of government where citizens elect people to represent them.
5. The Greeks invented these to build temples and other important buildings.
6. These people could win their freedom by fighting in the Coliseum.
7. The Romans invented these to provide strong support for buildings.
8. The name of the temple built to honor the goddess Athena.
9. This carried water from the mountains to the city.

Word Tree Posters

Word Tree Posters help students in grades 4 and up who are at the Derivational Relations stage of spelling development (Bear et al., 2000) to learn root words and their meanings. A Word Tree Poster can be created to last throughout the school year. The teacher creates a large tree to keep on the wall. Materials needed are velcro, word cards, and sentence strips. Each week, assign a student a new root to investigate. The student goes through steps 3, 4, and 6, placing the root meaning at the base of the tree and words with their definitions on the branches. Additional words students learn throughout the week can be added.

The procedures are as follows:
1. Select a root.
2. Share with each other as many word forms of this root as possible.
3. Use the dictionary and the suffixes and prefixes you know to find new words that you did not think of before.
4. Write the words and a short definition for each using the meaning of the root in your definitions.
5. Draw an outline of a tree.
6. Write the root at the base of the tree and each new word and its definition on individual branches.

A Sample Word Tree Poster for the Latin Root *'dic'* and a list of possible high-frequency roots:

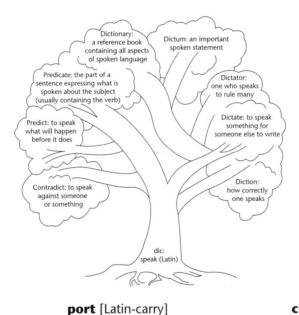

spec [Latin-see]   **port** [Latin-carry]   **cred** [Latin-believe]
graph [Greek-write]   **man** [Latin-hand]   **photo** [Greek-light]
rupt [Latin-break]   **script** [Latin-write]   **tract** [Latin-pull, drag]
dic [Latin-speak]   **vid** [Latin-see]   **fac** [Latin-make, do]
ped [Latin-foot]   **gram** [Greek-letter, write]   **therm** [Greek-heat]
loc [Latin-place]   **phon** [Greek-sound]   **mot** [Latin-move]
cycl [Greek-circle, ring] **aud** [Latin-hear]

Adapted from: Bear, D., Invernizzi, M., Templeton, S., & Johnson, F. (2000). *Words their way.* (2nd Ed.). Upper Saddle River, NJ: Prentice Hall.

Vocabulary Self-Selection (VSS) Chart

VSS charts help students "collect" vocabulary words that may pose a problem for them as they read narrative and expository texts. It is essential that with the VSS chart, **students select** the words that they do not know or words they want to learn. The teacher does not pre-select the words. The charts can focus on one specific book, on one particular chapter in a textbook, or the chart can be used as children read and work from a variety of sources. For example, the VSS below is focused on the book *Amos and Boris* by William Steig. A child may collect words and complete the chart as a before, during, or after reading activity.

Word	Word Parts	Meaning of Word Part(s)	Definition of the Word	Sentence with the Word
telescope	tele	tele—distant; far off	Instrument used to make far away things look closer	Amos used a telescope to see things that were far off in the distance.
luminous	lumin ous	lumin—light ous—full of	Full of light	The ocean looked luminous from the moonlight.

The example below is one that may be used as children select words from multiple texts.

Word	Book	Word Parts	Meaning of Word Parts	Definition of the Word	Sentence with the Word
telescope	Amos and Boris	tele—	Distant; far off	Instrument used to make far away things look closer.	Amos used a telescope to see things far off in the distance.
metamorphosis	Science	meta morph sis	meta—after morph—change, shape sis-the act of	A change in form or shape	Caterpillars go through metamorphosis as they change into a butterfly.

Adapted from: Haggard, M.R. (1986). The vocabulary self-selection strategy: Using student interest and word knowledge to enhance vocabulary growth. *Journal of Reading, 29* (7), 634–642.

Thematic Word Walls

An instructional technique developed and presented by Kay Brailler (Fresno, California, 8/1996) and modified by Jared J. Kaiser (2004), **thematic word walls** are a great adaptation of the traditional word wall. Index cards are arranged to spell out a word central to the topic or theme the class is studying (e.g. FRIENDS, AMERICAN INDIAN TRIBES, MYSTERY, etc.). Each letter of the theme word is made up of student-created cards on which words have been written that are collections from the students' background knowledge of the theme (e.g. when describing "mystery" characters, they may write *evil* and *hideous*; when thinking of description of "mystery" feelings, they may say *brave* or *embarrassed*.). As they read, they collect additional words for the wall. When the wall is sorted by parts of speech, the students consider picking verbs for one letter, adjectives for another, and adverbs for a third. The border surrounds the large theme word and is made up of an alphabetical list of theme-related nouns with matching pictures. The entire word wall is 3 feet high and ranges from 15–20 feet long, depending on the length of the theme word. Students gain a sense of ownership for the word wall and tend to use the words in their writing. The teacher may ask students to choose specific types of words, such as multisyllabic words, nouns, adjectives, root words, suffixes, etc.

Sample Letter "M" from MYSTERY Thematic Word Wall

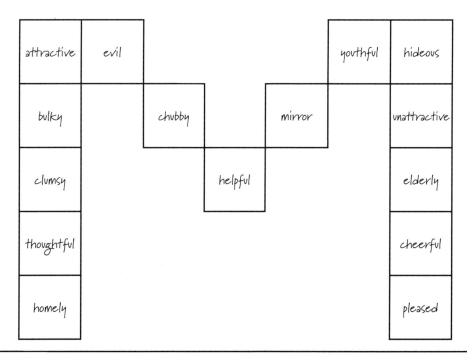

From Tompkins, Gail E., & Cathy L. Blanchfield. *Teaching Vocabulary: 50 Creative Strategies, Grades K–12,* 1/e Published by Allyn and Bacon/Merrill Education, Boston, MA. Copyright © 2004 by Pearson Education. Reprinted by permission of the publisher.

Samples of Student-Chosen Words for MYSTERY Thematic Word Wall

(each word written on a card which is used to create the letter which, when combined, creates the word MYSTERY)

M—adjectives describing characters found in mysteries [attractive, bulky, cheerful, chubby, clever, clumsy, devious, elderly, evil, grumpy, helpful, hideous, homely, minor, pleased, quaint, rude, snoopy, thoughtful, unattractive, youthful]

Y—adjectives describing the setting found in mysteries [ancient, bustling, chilly, delightful, dark, stormy, dismal, foggy, gigantic, quaint, rainy]

S—adverbs used in mysteries [argumentatively, carefully, cautiously, differently, excitingly, friendly, hopefully, lovely, peacefully, quickly, roughly, safely, slowly, smoothly, suspiciously]

T—adjectives describing feelings in mysteries [brave, depressed, disagreeable, downhearted, embarrassed, humiliated, mortified, melancholy, satisfied, timid, uncomfortable, vexed]

E—adjectives describing a person's body [bald, buff, chubby, considerable, fat, healthy, mighty, muscular, slim, strong, tremendous, unhealthy, wrinkly]

R—words having the suffix CIAN, which means 'having a certain skill or art' [beautician, dietician, electrician, logician, magician, mathematician, mortician, musician, optician, patrician, physician, pediatrician, pyrotechnician, technician]

Y—words containing the root DUC, DUCE, or DUCT which comes from the Latin *ducere*, meaning *'to lead'* [abduct, aqueduct, conductive, educate, introduction, product, reduce, reduction]

The Border—alphabetical lists of nouns related to a mystery [alligator, bridle, candlestick, Dalmation, ermine, fright, giant, helicopter, iguana, juggler, karate, letter, magazine, nicotine, octopus, passageway, quicksand, revolver, sickle, telephone, unicorn, vegetable, wreckage, x-ray, yawl, zodiac, anaconda, butler, calumet, denture, enclosure, fireworks, gumshoe, hickory nuts, immortal, janitor, kingfisher, lobster, magnet, Napoleon, Oxford, paddle, quail, rascal, saxophone, timepiece, umbrella, victim, wolf, x-files, yacht, zero]

Example of a Thematic Word Wall for MYSTERY

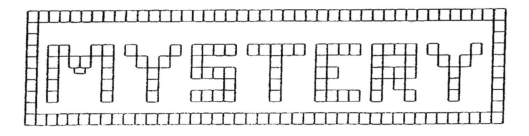

From Tompkins, Gail E., & Cathy L. Blanchfield. *Teaching Vocabulary: 50 Creative Strategies, Grades K–12*, 1/e Published by Allyn and Bacon/Merrill Education, Boston, MA. Copyright © 2004 by Pearson Education. Reprinted by permission of the publisher.

Possible Sentences

Possible Sentences (Moore & Moore, 1986) combines a vocabulary study with a prediction activity to acquaint students with new vocabulary in the text to be read, support them as they verify the accuracy of the possible statements they create, and generate curiosity for the text to be read. Possible sentences can be used for narrative and expository texts and is best when unfamiliar words are mixed with familiar vocabulary. **Five steps** are followed in the possible sentence activity:

1. **List key vocabulary words from the text** [The teacher selects key vocabulary terms from the content area textbook or narrative piece. Approximately 6–8 for beginning or striving readers; 10–15 for average and proficient readers. These terms should reflect the key concepts of the text or vocabulary knowledge needed to support comprehension.]

2. **Elicit sentences from students** [Display the words on the chalkboard, chart paper, or overhead. Ask students to pronounce each word after the teacher.]

3. **Read the text to verify generated sentences** [Ask students to compose a sentence that they think could possibly be found in the text for each word. Stress that the sentences must not be personal in nature. In other words, students should avoid sentences such as "I use a *compass* when I go hiking." Rather, the sentences should reflect the type of sentences they would find in a textbook, if expository, or narrative story. Write each sentence exactly as dictated by the students, even though they may be inaccurate. Continue with the process until the students are not able to generate any more sentences.]

4. **Evaluate the sentences** [Ask students to read the assigned selection using the generated sentences as their guides. They read to either confirm or refute the information included in their possible sentences. On a sheet numbered from 1–8 or 1–15 (depending on how many sentences were generated), students write a 'T' next to any generated sentences that they believe are **true**, an 'F' next to any generated sentences that they think are **false**, and a 'DK' next to those they are not sure whether they are true or false.]

5. **Create new sentences** [As a whole class or in small groups, have students revise the generated sentences to reflect the way the vocabulary words were used in the text that was read. In other words, students rewrite the sentences to make them true, reflecting how the words were used in the text.

A sample possible sentence format may look like this:

1. Key concepts/vocabulary word list
compass   luminous   breakers

2. Student-generated possible sentences (before reading) and student reactions (after reading)
T (True), F (False), DK (Don't Know)
  T   **1.** The scout master used a compass to find his way through the forest.
  T   **2.** The moonlight was so luminous the soldiers could see their way at night.
  F   **3.** The breakers in the fuse box need to be switched so the power can be turned on.

3. Modified sentences (after reading)
  1. ——
  2. ——
  3. He liked the waves and the rolling breakers as they crashed ashore on the beach.

From Readence, J.E., Moore, D.W., and Rickelman, R.J. *Prereading Activities for Content Area Reading and Learning,* Newark, DE: International Reading Association.

Contextual Redefinition

Contextual redefinition is an excellent instructional technique for reviewing and integrating word analysis strategies. This technique aids students in the use of context clues by contrasting definitions from words in isolation and words in context (Tierney & Readence, 2000). It provides reinforcement for dictionary skills as well. It is effective, yet easy to implement. It consists of the following steps:

1. Choosing hard words
- Words are chosen that are important to an understanding of the selection and which may pose problems for students.

2. Presenting words in isolation
- Unfamiliar words are listed on the chalkboard or transparency. Volunteers are invited to pronounce them—they are given help if needed—and are asked to define the words. Because the words are presented in isolation, students must rely on morphemic analysis clues to define the words. Students provide reasons for their definitions; however, because they have little to go on, their proposed definitions may be quite off the mark. Encourage students to agree on one meaning for each word.
- **Example word:** *vivacious*

3. Presenting words in context
- Words are then presented in context. Ideally, this would be the context in which the words are used in the selection to be read: *"In contrast to her more serious husband, Mary Todd Lincoln was a vivacious and colorful addition to the Washington scene"* (Burchard, 1999, p.49). However, if the context is not adequate, create your own sentence. Using the context, students, in pairs or groups, make their best guesses about the meaning of each word. They are expected to explain why they constructed a particular meaning. This gives them opportunity to share their reasoning processes. The group again must agree on one meaning for each word.

4. Checking the meaning in the dictionary
- Students look up the word in the dictionary and discuss possible definitions with the group. The group chooses the most appropriate definition.
- **Example:** In deriving the meaning of *vivacious*, students use their knowledge of the root *viv* [life] and the suffix *ous* [full of], the context clue, and the dictionary definition to construct a meaning of the word, *full of life.*

Contextual redefinition provides a natural way to provide guided practice in three interrelated word identification skills: **morphemic analysis, contextual analysis,** and **dictionary usage.** The procedure helps students to arrive at a fuller, more precise understanding of words.

From Readence, J.E., Moore, D.W., and Rickelman, R.J. *Prereading Activities for Content Area Reading and Learning,* Newark, DE: International Reading Association.

Analogies

Analogies are important for vocabulary development because they help children see relationships between words. They are also found in many standardized tests.

There are different types of analogies:

1. **part to whole** [clutch: transmission:: key:_____] (starter, engine, exhaust)
2. **person to situation** [Lincoln: slavery::_____: independence] (Jefferson, Kennedy, Jackson)
3. **cause and effect** [CB: radio reception:: television:_____] (eating, homework, gym)
4. **synonym** [bourgeoisie: middle class:: proletariat:_____] (upper class, lower class, royalty)
5. **antonym** [pinch: handful:: sip:_____] (pet, gulp, taste)
6. **geography** [Everest: Matterhorn::_____: Alps] (Ozarks, Andes, Himalayas)
7. **measurement** [minutes: clock::_____: temperature] (liters, degrees, gradations)
8. **time** [24 hours: rotation:: 365 days:_____] (Eastern time, revolution, axis)

Type examples reprinted from:
Vacca, R.T. & Vacca, J.L. (1996). *Content area reading* (5th Ed.). New York: HarperCollins.

The example below is a format that can be used for primary grade students that shows the use of words instead of using the single colon (meaning "is to") and double colon (meaning "as"). Once children have become familiar with analogies, then the words "is to" and "as" should be replaced with the colon and double colon. Also, after children have become experienced in doing analogies, answer choices can be eliminated in order to provide opportunities for children to come up with their own answers without prompts.

1. Hot is to cold as day is to _____.
   up   night   long

2. Dog is to cat as small is to _____.
   little   big   short

3. Puppy is to _____ as young is to old.
   playful   dog   kitten

4. _____ is to white as on is to off.
   Red   Black   Door

5. Happy is to _____ as stop is to go.
   glad   sad   frown

6. Slow is to _____ as long is to short.
   silly   happy   fast

Prefixes and Their Meanings

A **prefix** is a morpheme that comes at the beginning of a root word or base word. A prefix carries meaning.

Prefix	Meaning	Sample Word(s)
1. a, an	Without	Anaerobic
2. ab	Away, from	Abnormal
3. ad	To, toward	Adhere
4. aero	Air	Aerobic
5. ambi, amphi	Both	Ambidextrous
6. ante	Before	Antebellum
7. anti	Against, opposite	Antibiotic
8. auto	Self	Autobiography, automobile
9. be	Make	Belittle
10. bene, bon	Good	Beneficiary, benefactor
11. bi	Two	Biped
12. bio	Life	Biology, biography
13. circum	Around	Circumnavigate
14. com, con, co	Together, with	Combine, co-exist, commune
15. chrono	Time	Chronology
16. contra, contro	Against	Contradict
17. di, dis	Two	Dissect
18. de	Out of, reverse, away	Deport, desegregate
19. deci	Ten	Decibels, decimal
20. demi	Half	Demitasse
21. dis	Not	Dislike, distrust
22. dia	Through, across	Dialect, diameter
23. dys	Abnormal, bad	Dysfunctional, dystrophy
24. ex, e	Out, from, out of, prior to	Excrete, exit, expel
25. extra, extro	Outside, beyond	Extraterrestrial
26. geo	Earth	Geology
27. gen	Race, kind	Generation
28. hyper	Over, excess	Hyperactive
		continues

List compiled by Alice Snyder, 1997.

Prefix	Meaning	Sample Word(s)
29. hypo	Under, less	Hypoactive
30. homo	Same, alike	Homogeneous
31. hetero	Mixed	Heterogeneous
32. hemi	Half	hemisphere
33. in	Not	Inactive, incapable
34. in, en	Into	Inbreed, endure
35. inter	Between	Interstate, interact
36. intra	Within	Intrastate
37. iso	Equal	Isometric
38. macro	Large	Macroscopic
39. micro	Small	Microscopic, microbe
40. mega	Huge	Megaphone, megabucks
41. magni	Great, large	Magnify
42. meta	Change, beyond	Metamorphosis
43. mono	One	Monogram, monologue
44. mis	Bad, badly, wrong, wrongly	Misdiagnose, mislead
45. multi	Many	Multilingual
46. neo	New, recent	Neonatal
47. non	Not	Nonalchoholic, nonabrasive
48. octo	Eight	Octopus, octagon
49. omni	All	Omnipresent, omniferous
50. ortho	Straight	Orthotics, orthodontics
51. osteo	Bone	Osteoporosis
52. over	Above, beyond	Overdue, overflow
53. pedi, pod	Foot, footed	Podiatrist, pedal
54. pan	All	Panorama, pandemic
55. para	Beside, near, beyond	Paranormal, paralegal

Prefix	Meaning	Sample Word(s)
56. per	Through	Permeate
57. phono	Sound, voice	Phonograph
58. photo	Light	Photograph
59. poly	Many, much	Polygon, polygamist
60. pos, pon	Place, put	Position
61. post	After	Postnatal, postdate
62. pre	Before	Preview, predate, prehistoric
63. pro	For, forward	Procreate, proactive
64. pseudo	False	Pseudonym
65. psycho	Mind	Psychology
66. quad	Four	Quadrilateral
67. retro	Backward	Retroactive, retrospective
68. semi	Half	Semicircle
69. sub	Under	Submarine, subversive
70. syn, sym	Together, with	Synthesis, symphony
71. super	Over, above, beyond	Superimpose, supervise
72. tele	Far, distant	Telescope, telephone
73. ten	To hold	Tenacious, tentacles
74. thermo	Heat	Thermometer
75. trans	Across	Transcontinental, transient
76. un	Not	Undeveloped, undo
77. under	Below	Understate, underwear
78. uni	One	Unicycle
79. vita	Life	Vitality, vitamin
80. zoo	Animal	Zoology

Root Words and Their Meanings

Root words are morphemes that cannot stand alone. They need additional word parts added to them in order to form a complete word in English. Roots have origins in various languages, such as French, Latin, Greek, Old English, etc.

Root	Meaning	Sample Word(s)
1. ac	Sharp	acupuncture
2. agog	Leader	pedagogue
3. agri	Field	agriculture
4. ali	Another	alimony
5. alter	Other	altercation
6. am	Love	amity, amnesty
7. anim	Mind, soul	animosity, anisism
8. ann, enn	Year	annual, perennial
9. anthrop	Man	anthropology
10. aqua, aque	Water	aqueduct
11. arch	Ruler, first	archbishop
12. aster	Star	asteroid
13. aud	Hear	auditory
14. auto	Self	autonomous
15. belli	War	belligerent
16. ben	Good	benevolent
17. biblio	Book	bibliography
18. bio	Life	biology, autobiography
19. breve	Short	brevity, abbreviate
20. cap	To take	capture, captivate
21. cess	To yield, to go	incessant
22. cent	One hundred	centenary, century
23. chron	Time	chronological, synchronize
24. cid, cis	To cut, to kill	fratricide, homicide, scissors
25. cit	To call, to start	citation, incite
26. clam	To cry out	exclamatory, exclaim
27. cognit	To learn	cognition, recognize
28. corpor	Body	corporation, corporal

List compiled by Alice Snyder, 1997.

29. da, dat	To give	data
30. dic, dict	To say	dictation, diction
31. doc, doct	To teach	doctrine, indoctrinate
32. dynamo	Power, strength	dynamic, dynamite
33. err	To wander	erroneous, erratic
34. fall, fals	To deceive	falsify
35. fid	Belief, faith	fidelity, confidence
36. frag, fract	To break	fracture, fragment
37. gam	Marriage	monogamy, polygamy
38. grad	Go, step	gradual, graduate, gradation
39. gram	Writing	telegram, monogram
40. gress	Go, step	transgress, Congress, progression
41. it	Journey	itinerant, itinerary
42. liber	Book	library, librarian
43. logu	To talk	dialogue, monologue
44. luc	Light	lucent, luciferous, translucent
45. magn	Great	magnify, magnificent, magnanimous
46. man	Hand	emancipate, magnanimous
47. mon, monit	To warn	premonition, monitor
48. morph	Shape, form	morphology, metamorphosis
49. nat	Born	prenatal, nativity
50. nov	New	novice, novelty
51. omni	All	omniferous
52. pac	Peace	pacify
53. pater, part	Father	paternity, patriarch
54. ped, pud	Foot	pedestrian, pedal
55. phil	Love	philanthropist, philosophy
56. psych	Mind	psychiatrist, psychology
57. ques, quir	To ask	question, queries, inquiry
58. rid, ris	Laugh	ridiculous, ridicule
59. rupt	To break, lender	disruption, corrupt
60. sci	To know	science
61. sect	To cut	section, dissect
62. sequi, secut	To follow	sequel, sequence
63. tempro	Time	temporary, temporal
64. therm	Heat	thermos, thermometer
65. urb	City	suburb, urban
66. vac	Empty	vacuum, evacuate, vacant
67. vid, vis	To see	evident, visible
68. viv, vit	Alive	vivify, vivacious
69. vol	Wish	volition, voluntary
70. volv, volut	To roll	revolution, evolve

Suffixes and Their Meanings

A **suffix** is a morpheme that is placed at the end of a root word or base word. A suffix carries meaning.

Root	Meaning	Example Words
1. able, ible	Capable of	Intangible—not capable of being touched or reached Plausible—capable of being trusted Reprehensible—blamable
2. ac, ic	Like, pertaining to	Eclectic—choosing ideas, methods from various sources Dogmatic—opinionated; having opinions without proof Lethargic—like having a lack of energy
3. ant	One who	Assistant—one who assists
4. ar	One who	Liar—one who lies
5. arium	Place for	Aquarium—a place for fish or other water life
6. tude	State of	Certitude—state of being sure, certain Gratitude—state of being thankful, gracious
7. ary	Like, connected with	Adversary—opponent; one who opposes or resists Arbitrary—proceeding from a whim or fancy
8. ation	The act of	Imputation—the act of accusation Approbation—the act of praising, commending Adulation—flattering and giving excessive praise
9. ous	Full of	Ludicrous—absurd; ridiculous Facetious—full of joking Malodorous—full of unpleasant odor
10. eer, er, or	Person who	Conductor—a person who leads, conducts, manages Censor—a person who finds faults; an adverse critic Slanderer—a person who gives false information about another person which is damaging in nature
11. ent	One who	Resident—one who resides or lives
12. ling	Small	Fledgling—a small bird or baby chicken
13. escent	Becoming	Obsolescent—becoming obsolete; going out of use or style Iridescent—becoming colorful like the rainbow
14. fic	Making, doing	Horrific—to make horrifying Omnific—all-creating
15. fy	To make	Rectify—to make better a situation that was created by the person who caused the problem Vivify—to make vivid; to enliven

16. iferous	Producing, bearing	Vociferous—producing loud, noisy outcries to make one's own feelings known Coniferous—bearing or producing cones
17. il, ile	Capable of	Puerile—childish; silly; immature Docile—easy to manage or discipline
18. ism	Doctrine, belief	Monotheism—belief that there is only one God Misoneism—hatred of anything new
19. ist	Dealer, doer	Anarchist—someone who believes in and promotes anarchy or lack of rule or government Antagonist—someone who opposes or competes with another; opponent
20. ity	State of being	Fidelity—state of being faithful
21. ive	Like	Pensive—thoughtful in a sad way; melancholy Apprehensive—fearful of what may come
22. oid	Resembling	Crystalloid—resembling crystal Anthropoid—resembling man; manlike
23. osis	Condition	Neurosis—psychic or mental disorder of such conditions as phobias, depression, anxiety Symbiosis—two unlike organisms living together in mutually helpful association
24. y	State of	Sunny—state of having lots of sunshine
25. ology	Study of	Mythology—the study of mythical stories Anthropology—the study of man
26. ness	State of being	Happiness—state of being happy
27. less	Without	Penniless—without money
28. ery, ry	Products	Pottery—products made from clay
29. ful	Full of	Mouthful—mouth is full of
30. ess	One who (female)	Actress—woman who acts
31. ish	Of or belonging to a nationality; like or characteristic of; verging on; somewhat, rather; about; ending on some verbs from French verb origins	Spanish; boyish; bookish; tallish, bluish; thirtyish; finish (finir), punish (punir)

List compiled by Alice Snyder, 1997.

Chapter Three

Strategies for Teaching Phonics, Syllabication, Decoding, and Fluency

The Names Test
Protocol Sheet

Purpose: To determine a student's ability to apply phonics generalizations as he/she attacks unknown words. The teacher analyzes each child's decoding errors and categorizes them based on given phonics categories where the greatest number of errors occurred. Subsequent individual or small group instruction in these areas is planned and delivered.

Name _____ **Grade** _____ **Teacher** _____ **Date** _____

Directions: Pretend you are a teacher. It's the first day of school. This is a list of the students in your class. Read aloud the list of students' names.

Jay Conway	Tim Cornell	Chuck Hoke	Yolanda Clark
Kimberly Blake	Roberta Slade	Homer Preston	Gus Quincy
Cindy Sampson	Chester Wright	Ginger Yale	Patrick Tweed
Stanley Shaw	Wendy Swain	Glen Spencer	Fred Sherwood
Flo Thornton	Dee Skidmore	Grace Brewster	Ned Westmoreland
Ron Smitherman	Troy Whitlock	Vance Middleton	Zane Anderson
Bernard Pendergraph	Shane Fletcher	Floyd Sheldon	Dean Baterman
Austin Shepherd	Bertha Dale	Neal Wade	Jake Murphy
Joan Brooks	Gene Loomis	Thelma Rinehart	

Adapted from Cunningham, P.M. (1990, October). The Names Test: A quick assessment of decoding ability. *The Reading Teacher, 44*(2), 124–129. Copyright 1990 by the International Reading Association (www.reading.org).

The Names Test Record Sheet

Jay Conway	Tim Cornell	Chuck Hoke	Yolanda Clark
Kimberly Blake	Roberta Slade	Homer Preston	Gus Quincy
Cindy Sampson	Chester Wright	Ginger Yale	Patrick Tweed
Stanley Shaw	Wendy Swain	Glen Spencer	Fred Sherwood
Flo Thornton	Dee Skidmore	Grace Brewster	Ned Westmoreland
Ron Smitherman	Troy Whitlock	Vance Middleton	Zane Anderson
Bernard Pendergraph	Shane Fletcher	Floyd Sheldon	Dean Baterman
Austin Shepherd	Bertha Dale	Neal Wade	Jake Murphy
Joan Brooks	Gene Loomis	Thelma Rinehart	

Phonics Category	Errors
Initial Consonants	/37
Initial Consonant Blends	/21
Consonant Digraphs	/15
Short Vowels	/36
Long Vowels/VC-final e	/23
Vowel Digraphs	/15
Controlled Vowels	/25
Schwa	/15

Adapted from Cunningham, P.M. (1990, October). The Names Test: A quick assessment of decoding ability. *The Reading Teacher*, 44(2), 124–129. Copyright 1990 by the International Reading Association (www.reading.org).

The Names Test Sample Student Protocol

Name _____ **Grade** _____ **Teacher** _____ **Date** _____

Phonics Category	Errors
Initial Consonants	1/37
Initial Consonant Blends	1/21
Consonant Digraphs	3/15
Short Vowels	2/36
Long Vowels/VC-final e	*8/23
Vowel Digraphs	*5/15
Controlled Vowels	*7/25
Schwa	1/15

Conver ✓
Jay Conway

✓
Kimberly Blake

Kindy ✓
Cindy Sampson

Wendell Swan ✓
Stanley Shaw

Floy Thonton ✓
Flo Thornton

✓
Ron Smitherman

Bamid   Pedugraph
Bernard Pendergraph

Astin ✓
Austin Shepherd

John ✓
Joan Brooks

✓
Chuck Hoke

Robert ✓
Roberta Slade

Ging   Yell
Ginger Yale

✓
Glen Spencer

Bowster
Grace Brewster

✓
Vance Middleton

✓
Floyd Sheldon

Berta ✓
Bertha Dale

Glen ✓
Gene Loomis

Carnell ✓
Tim Cornell

✓
Homer Preston

✓
Chester Wright

✓
Dee Skidmore

✓
Troy Whitlock

✓
Shane Fletcher

Nel ✓
Neal Wade

Temla   Rainhart
Thelma Rinehart

Yondolada ✓
Yolanda Clark

✓   *Quancy*
Gus Quincy

✓
Patrick Tweed

Steward ✓
Fred Sherwood

✓
Ned Westmoreland

✓
Zane Anderson

Batman
Dean Baterman

✓
Jake Murphy

Adapted from Cunningham, P.M. (1990, October). The Names Test: A quick assessment of decoding ability. *The Reading Teacher, 44*(2), 124–129. Copyright 1990 by the International Reading Association (www.reading.org)

Scoring Matrix for the Names Test (p. 1)

Name _____

Date _____

Name	InCon	InConBl	ConDig	ShVow	LongVow/VC-e	VowDig	Con Vow	Schwa
Jay	J					ay		
Conway	C			o		ay		
Tim	T			i				
Cornell	C			e			or	
Chuck			Ch	u				
Hoke	H				oke			
Yolanda	Y			a	o			a
Clark		Cl					ar	
Kimberly	K			i	y		er	
Blake		Bl			ake			
Roberta	R				o		er	a
Slade		Sl			ade			
Homer	H				o		er	
Preston		Pr		e				o
Gus	G			u				
Quincy		Kw		i	y			
Cindy	C			i	y			
Sampson	S			a				o

Name	InCon	InConBl	ConDig	ShVow	LongVow/VC-e	VowDig	Con Vow	Schwa
Chester			Ch	e			er	
Wright	Wr				i			
Ginger	G			i			er	
Yale	Y				ale			
Patrick	P			a, i				
Tweed		Tw				ee		
Stanley		St		a		ey		
Shaw			Sh				aw	
Wendy	W			e	y			
Swain		Sw					ai	
Glen		Gl		e				
Spencer		Sp		e			er	
Fred		Fr		e				
Sherwood			Sh			oo	er	
Flo		Fl			o			
Thornton			Th				or	o
Bernard	B						er, ar	
Pendergraph	P		ph	e, a			er	

Adapted from Cunningham, P.M. (1990, October). The Names Test: A quick assessment of decoding ability. *The Reading Teacher, 44*(2), 124–129. Copyright 1990 by the International Reading Association (www.reading.org)

Scoring Matrix for the Names Test (p. 2)

Name_____   Date_____

Name	InCon	InConBl	ConDig	ShVow	LongVow/VC-e	VowDig	ConVow	Schwa
Dee	D					ee		
Skidmore		Sk		i			or	
Grace		Gr			ace			
Brewster		Br					ew, er	
Ned	N			e				
Westmoreland	W			e			or	a
Ron	R			o				
Smitherman		Sm	th	i			er	a
Troy		Tr				oy		
Whitlock			Wh	i, o				
Vance	V			a				
Middleton	M			i				o
Zane	Z				ane			
Anderson				a			er	o
Shane			Sh		ane			
Fletcher		Fl	ch	e			er	
Floyd		Fl				oy		
Sheldon			Sh	e				o

Name	InCon	InConBl	ConDig	ShVow	LongVow/VC-e	VowDig	ConVow	Schwa
Dean	D					ea		
Bateman	B				ate			a
Thelma			Th	e				a
Rinehart	R				ine		ar	
Austin						Au		i
Shepherd			Sh	e			er	
Bertha	B		th				er	a
Dale	D				ale			
Neal	N					ea		
Wade	W				ade			
Jake	J				ake			
Murphy	M		ph		y		ur	
Joan	J					oa		
Brooks		Br				oo		
Gene	G				ene			
Loomis	L					oo		i

Adapted from Cunningham, P.M. (1990, October). The Names Test: A quick assessment of decoding ability. *The Reading Teacher, 44*(2), 124–129. Copyright 1990 by the International Reading Association (www.reading.org)

Stages of Spelling Development

Level 1—Precommunicative Stage

The word "precommunicative" is used to describe a child's writing before it can be read by people other than the child who wrote it. At this stage, the child conveys a message through his or her scribbles, shapes, drawing and/or letters that are strung together randomly. At this stage, the child does NOT know that letters represent sounds.

Examples of precommunicative "spelling"   T L S—bike   P T R F—dress

Level 2—Semiphonetic Stage

Semiphonetic spellers recognize that letters say sounds; they realize that there is a relationship between letters and sounds. The word "semiphonetic" is used to indicate that these spellers write only some of the letters in a word. Most often, they use the initial consonant to represent a whole word. Students tend to spell by sound, often using consonants. They may or may not put spaces between words. At this stage, teachers should teach phonetic strategies.

Examples of semiphonetic "spelling"   K—cake   B—bike   T—type
M B E W W M L N T—My baby was with me last night.

Level 3—Phonetic Stage

Phonetic spellers spell words the way they sound to them. They write all the sounds **they hear** in words. These spellings do not necessarily look like English spelling, but they are quite readable (and make sense). Initial and final consonants are in place and these spellers gradually add vowels, even though they may not be correct. Word spacing is evident. Teachers should ensure that visual strategies are included in their program.

Examples of phonetic "spelling"   tak—take tip—type   It trd in to a brd. (It turned into a bird.)

Level 4—Transitional Stage

Transitional spellers begin to write words in a more conventional way. They are making a transition from relying on **sound** as they spell to a reliance on **visual memory** of how the word looks in print. Students have learned about letter patterns but often use them incorrectly. They write with more correct vowels in every syllable. Often all the letters needed to spell the word are there, but they may reverse some letters. Visual strategies and morphemic strategies should form the major part of the teaching program for students at this stage of spelling development.

Examples of transitional "spelling"   tipe—type   taek—take   muose—mouse   opne—open

Level 5—Conventional Stage

Conventional spellers develop over years of word study, reading, and writing. Knowledge of the English spelling system is firmly established. These spellers know when words do not look right and they experiment with alternatives. They spell a large number of words automatically. Conventional spelling is a lifelong process. We will always encounter words we will not know how to spell automatically.

Reprinted with permission from *Teaching Kids to Spell* by J. Richard Gentry & Jean Wallace Gillet. Copyright © 1993 by Richard Gentry and Jean Wallace Gillet. Published by Heinemann, Portsmouth, NH. All rights reserved.

Gentry Developmental Spelling Test

Early Years K–8
(May 1985)
Dr. J. Richard Gentry
Professor of Elementary Education and Reading
Western Carolina University

Having an awareness of students' developmental spelling progress enables a teacher to respond intelligently and to make sound instructional decisions as children progress toward spelling proficiency. A good place to begin gaining a better understanding of the developmental spelling process is to administer a developmental spelling test.

Administering the Gentry Developmental Spelling Test

The test is designed for students in elementary grades. When administering the test, you will obtain spellings that can be categorized into five developmental spelling stages: precommunicative, semiphonetic, phonetic, transitional, and conventional.

Follow these directions: Explain to the child that the words may be too difficult for him/her to spell, but you want the child to invent or use his/her best guess at what the spelling might be. Explain that the activity will not be graded as right or wrong, but that it will be used to see how he/she **thinks** certain words should be spelled. Be encouraging and make the activity challenging and fun.

Call out each word, give the sentence provided, and call out the word again.

	WORD LIST	
1.	monster	The boy was eaten by a MONSTER.
2.	united	You live in the UNITED States.
3.	dress	The girl wore a new DRESS.
4.	bottom	A big fish lives at the BOTTOM of the lake.
5.	hiked	We HIKED to the top of the mountain.
6.	human	Miss Piggy is not a HUMAN.
7.	eagle	An EAGLE is a powerful bird.
8.	closed	The little girl CLOSED the door.
9.	bumped	The car BUMPED into the bus.
10.	type	TYPE the letter on the typewriter.
Alternative word for	7. beagle	A BEAGLE is a nice dog.

Developmental Spelling Test Scoring Chart
Dr. J. Richard Gentry
Professor of Elementary Education and Reading
Western Carolina University

Words	Precommunicative	Semiphonetic	Phonetic	Transitional	Conventional
1. monster	random letters	mtr	mostr	monster	monster
2. united	random letters	u	unitd	younighted	united
3. dress	random letters	jrs	jras	dres	dress
4. bottom	random letters	bt	bodm	bottum	bottom
5. hiked	random letters	h	hikt	hicked	hiked
6. human	random letters	um	humm	humun	human
7. eagle	random letters	el	egl	egul	eagle
8. closed	random letters	kd	klosd	clossed	closed
9. bumped	random letters	b	bopt	bumpped	bumped
10. type	random letters	tp	tip	tipe	type

Developmental Spelling Test Scoring Chart

Dr. J. Richard Gentry
Professor of Elementary Education and Reading
Western Carolina University

Words	Precommunicative	Semiphonetic	Phonetic	Transitional	Conventional
1. monster	random letters	mtr	mostr	monster	monster
2. united	random letters	u	unitd	younighted	united
3. dress	random letters	jrs	jras	dres	dress
4. bottom	random letters	bt	bodm	bottum	bottom
5. hiked	random letters	h	hikt	hicked	hiked
6. human	random letters	um	humm	humun	human
7. eagle	random letters	el	egl	egul	eagle
8. closed	random letters	kd	klosd	clossed	closed
9. bumped	random letters	b	bopt	bumpped	bumped
10. type	random letters	tp	tip	tipe	type

MoNStR   UNitD

DreS   BotM

HiKeD   HumN

EGLe   CoELSD

BuPt   Tipe

Developmental Writing Scale
Beginning Writers

READ DESCRIPTORS FOR EACH LEVEL OF THE BEGINNING WRITER'S SCALE FROM BOTTOM TO TOP

Level 8:   ___Child writes the start of a story.
___Mistakes in grammar, mechanics, and usage may detract from clarity and meaning.
___Child begins to use more conventional spelling.
___At least two thoughts follow one another in logical sequence.

Level 7:   ___Child begins to use capitalization and simple punctuation (e.g. period) often in a random fashion.
___Child uses both phonics and sight strategies to spell words.
___Child writes some sentences related to topic and some not related to topic.
___Child writes short, simple sentences that are not in a pattern form.
___Child writes sentences of more than 4 words following a pattern.

Level 6:   ___Child begins to write 2 or 3 sentences using a simple pattern form of 3 or 4 words (e.g. I love…).
___Child uses invented spelling and some conventional spelling.
___Child writes a single, factual, understandable sentence independently.

Level 5:   ___Child begins to use spaces between words.
___Child uses familiar words and invented spelling words to convey short, simple message.
___Child uses initial consonants to represent words.
___Child uses labels for his pictures.
___Child writes familiar words.

Level 4:   ___Child writes letters in word grouping and can read it back.
___Child writes letters to convey a message and can read it back.
___Child dictates one or more sentences, copies it, reads it back, and can still remember it the next day.
___Child dictates one or more sentences, copies it, and can read it back.
___Child dictates one or more sentences and copies it.**

Level 3:   ___Letters don't match sounds.
___Child writes alphabet letter strings.
___Child copies words he/she sees around the room.
___Copies dictated words.**

Level 2:   ___Alphabet letters and mock letters are in a line across the page.
___Child writes alphabet and mock letters around the page.
___Child writes mock letters.
___Child pretends to write.

Level 1:   ___Child draws a picture in response to a prompt and can verbalize about it.
___Child draws a picture and can talk about his picture.
___Child draws a picture, but cannot verbalize about picture.
___Child attempts to write in scribbles or draws patterns.
___Uncontrolled scribbling.   **[start here and read up]**

Please keep in mind that both the Beginning Writer's Scale and the Extending Writer's Scale (on the next page) are developmental and the child's writing may not demonstrate all the characteristics listed in a given level. For example, most, but not all descriptors of Level 7 (or Level 10, etc.) need apply to a piece for that piece to be considered a Level 7 (or 10, etc.). Teacher judgment is essential in deciding the level that best describes a certain piece. We have found that use of the descriptors in conjunction with use of the exemplars results in highly reliable scoring.

**Dictate: Child tells someone else what he wants to write. That person writes it for the child. The child then copies on his/her paper. Even though dictation doesn't take place during an independent writing sample collection, dictation is an important stage of development which occurs frequently during ongoing writing workshops.

Extending Writer's Scale
Descriptors for Conventions of Writing

(handwritten: 2-3   24   3-5)

Element	Level 9	Level 10	Level 11	Level 12	Level 13	Level 14
Organization	Piece has beginning and middle but weak ending	Piece has beginning, middle, but weak ending; paragraphs are organized around a topic sentence	Piece has beginning, middle, end; paragraphs organized around a topic sentence	Similar to previous level	→	Begins use of foreshadowing; builds suspense
Sentence structure	Run-on sentences, mostly short, simple sentences using "because" and noun-verb beginnings of sentences	Fewer run-on sentences; mostly short, simple sentences w/n-vb beginnings; 1 or a few complex sentences with dependent clauses	Short, simple sentences w/n-vb beginnings; some different sentence beginnings, Ex: Suddenly; some complex & compound sentences	Uses variety of sentences, statements, questions, and exclamations	Uses sentence structure to fit mood of piece	→
Mechanics; usage	Mistakes do not detract from meaning; uses some periods & capital letters	Consistent use of periods; sometimes use of quotation marks, exclamation pts; indents paragraphs	Consistent use of standard n-vb agreement; uses commas in a series	Consistent use of periods, question marks, capitals, including proper nouns	→	→
Logical sequence	Most or all thoughts follow logical sequence	Same as level 9	All thoughts follow a logical sequence	→	→	→
Focus	Piece is focused on one idea	→	→	→	→	→
Sense of time and place	Limited mostly to repeated use of 'then'	Uses other words to describe place & time, 'When we got to...' 'By the time we...'	→	→	Writer provides detailed, believable description of a given place and/or time	→
Details	Factual details using mostly noun phrases; sounds like a list	Some details are related to each other & seem to flow together	Begins to paint word pictures; details give story credibility, they support the time setting of story	→	→	→
Length	Essentially 1 paragraph	Usually more than one paragraph	→	→	Fully elaborated topic; longer & greater # of paragraphs, e.g. 5 or more	→
Narrator	Almost all in first person (I, me)	Some 3rd person narration (he/she)	→	→	→	→
Word choice	Very basic use of words, i.e. nouns, verbs	Beginning use of adjectives	Frequent use of adjectives	Effective word choice evokes creative use of lang; strengthens writer's message; use of a few advanced adj's and/or adverbs	Consistent use of advanced adjectives, adverbs, verbs, etc.	→
Use of dialogue	Not used	Begins to use dialogue but no use of quotation marks	Uses quotation marks correctly most of the time	→	→	Uses dialogue to advance plot & develop characters
Emotions/ Humor/ Imagery	None elicited	Some simple, original images used, i.e. "It looked like a castle"	Some sense of humor, sadness, or other emotions, i.e. "Her long lost buddy..."	Feeling tone maintained from beginning to end	→	→
Audience/ Engaging Reader	No sense of audience	Captures reader's interest at times but doesn't sustain it	Captures & sustains reader's interest	→	→	→

Reprinted by permission of Jean Winsand Estate.

93

An Analytic Phonics Lesson Using the Poem "The Tooter"

Procedure: "The Tooter" is a great poem that was popular in the United States during the late 1700s and early 1800s. It is a good poem to use for exploring some of the different spellings of the /o͞o/ phoneme. An analytic phonics lesson allows students to work from the whole to part and back to the whole. See below for a sample lesson using "The Tooter."

The Tooter

A tooter who tooted the flute
Tried to tutor two tutors to toot.
"Toot-toot!" said the tooters.
"Tut-tut!" said the tutor.
"It's harder to tutor...than toot!"
So he tooted to Kalamazoo,
Where he dreamt he was eating a shoe.
He awoke in the night
With a terrible fright
And found it was perfectly true!

Preparation: Copy the poem on chart paper or overhead transparency.

Step One: Ask students to choral read the poem along with you.

Step Two: Have students come up, one at a time, to underline words that have the /o͞o/ phoneme using a vis-à-vis pen or sharpie.

Step Three: Using a Word Sorting approach, have students sort the underlined words according to their spelling pattern (words spelled with [oo], [u], [u-consonant-silent e], [o], [oe], and [ue]).

Step Four: Ask students to think about other words they know that have the /o͞o/ phoneme spelled in the same way as the six spelling patterns represented in the poem. List them under the correct categories.

Step Five: Ask students to reread "The Tooter." Present another text that contains many of the same spelling patterns as the six presented in the poem. Ask students to identify the words with the spelling patterns learned from "The Tooter" and other spellings for the /o͞o/ phoneme, such as (ew).

Step Six: Encourage students to make note of words that have the /o͞o/ phoneme when they read other texts.

From *Moses Supposes His Toeses are Roses and Other Silly Old Rhymes* by N. Patz.

Word Sorting
(Grades 3-5)

Word Sorting is an effective strategy that is based on the cognitive function of categorizing items such as words, pictures, or objects, into groups according to their similarities. There are three types of word sorting tasks: **sound (auditory) sorts, spelling sorts,** and **concept (meaning) sorts.** With sound/auditory sorts, students are asked to categorize words, objects, or pictures according to similar sound features. With spelling sorts, they sort words according to how they look, in other words, according to the relationships between visual letter patterns, pronunciation, meaning units, and/or spelling and word origin. With concept/meaning sorts, students classify words, pictures, or objects according to how they go together based on semantic relationships. They categorize according to properties that are independent of pronunciation or spelling.

With each type of word sorting task, there are various characteristics or sub-types of sorts. They are:

Picture Sort—pictures or objects are sorted [Ex: pictures with carpenters' tools, cooking utensils, and farmers' tools are given to sort according to who uses them]

Word Sort—students sort cards with words on them [Ex: cards with words with various spellings of the long e sound /ē/ to be sorted based on their spellings]

Single Sort—sort items one time for a specific reason [Ex: sort words for schwa sounds]

Multiple Sort—set of items is sorted in several ways for different reasons and in different groups [Ex: sort words for past tense verbs and present tense verbs, then sort past tense verbs again for regular and irregular formation of past tense. Then sort past tense ending with 'd' or 'ed' into how these sound (/d/, /t/, or /id/)].

Open Sort—students decide categories for sorting, then organize words/objects/pictures into columns based on the categories they've chosen. Others attempt to solve the sort by making hypothesis about the features or categories.

Closed Sort—teacher decides what the categories will be and selects key words to head each category with one marked with a question mark. The sort only has one specific subset of known words.

Reprinted with permission from *Guiding Readers and Writers: Teaching Comprehension, Genre, and Content Literacy* by Irene C. Fountas and Gay SuPinnell. Published by Heinemann, Portsmouth, NH. All rights reserved.

Word Sorting
Sound Sort

Directions: Read the words below. Decide which words go together, based on their sound similarity and sort them accordingly and write them according to the groupings in which you think they belong.

spoil   powerful
destroy   compound
employment   grown
bough   amount
shout   now
annoyance   low
thought   fountain
tough   thousand
thrown   growl
cow   bowed
pillow   though
through   doily
toilet

Some of these words are **diphthongs** and some are not. Sort them according to those that you think are diphthongs (under the "yes" column) and those that you think are not diphthongs (under the "no" column).

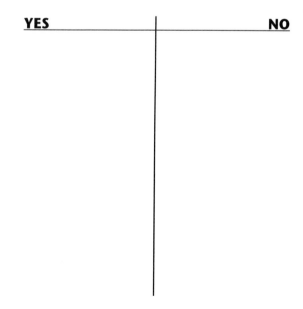

YES	**NO**

What do the words in the "yes" column have in common? What spelling patterns are common in these words? Based on what you've learned, what is a diphthong?

Inquiry-Based Syllabication
Partner Activity
Discovering a Generalization
about Dividing Words into Syllables

1. With a partner, examine the word cards in your pack. Sort them according to how you think they would be divided into syllables. Write the words here in your sorted lists.

2. After you sort your words, think of a generalization or a "rule" for dividing the words into syllables.

3. Write a sentence that describes the generalization (write the "rule" in your own words here).

4. Are there any exceptions? Brainstorm . . .

Set One	**Set Two**
promise	rapid
lizard	robot
medal	pirate
weather	confuse
meter	vacant
planet	honest
legal	hoping
even	comfort
cabin	problem
hotel	master
humid	sentence
solar	dessert
bacon	harvest
travel	hopping

Sample Inquiry-Based Spelling Lesson

Attacking a Problem of Sound-Alikes
–able and –ible

How do you know which ending to use, –able or –ible? There are clues to help you so you don't have to guess.

Clue 1:
Here is a group of words that end in –able. What is common about all of these words?

move, movable   use, usable   believe, believable
argue, arguable   live, livable   erase, erasable

What do you think the generalization might be relative to silent "e"? _____

_____

Clue 2:
Use what you learned from Clue 1 to decide the next generalization for using the –able ending.

advise_____   endure_____   peace_____

service_____   love_____   forgive_____

notice_____   conceive_____   manage_____

What do you think the next silent "e" generalization might be, based upon the words listed above?

_____

Clue 3:
There is another group of words that have a generalization you can discover for adding the –able suffix. All of the words have at least three syllables and have something in common which makes them a family. What do they have in common and what is the spelling generalization?

navigate, navigable   irritate, irritable   educate, educable

What is the generalization? _____

_____

Clue 4:
Now you know the generalization for words ending in –ate with three or more syllables, but what about the words which only have two syllables? Is there any difference?

debate, debatable   inflate, inflatable   rate, ratable

How do –ate words of only two syllables add –able? _____

_____

Therefore, the generalization about words that end in –ate is: Words of three or more syllables ending in –ate will drop _____ before adding –able. Words of only one or two syllables ending in –ate will drop only _____ before adding –able.

Now add –able appropriately to each of the following words.

appreciate_____   deflate_____

date_____   demonstrate_____

palate_____   explicate_____

tolerate_____   venerate_____

Now let's figure out which words end in –able and which in –ible.

Clue 5:
Look at several words ending in "y" and see whether you can figure out when you add –able and when you add –ible.

pay, payable   employ, employable   deny, deniable   envy, enviable

The generalization is: _____

_____

Clue 6:
These words also end in –able. What do they have in common?

avoidable, unavoidable   bearable, unbearable   blamable, unblamable

The generalization is _____

_____

Clue 7:
The following words give you a clue to adding –ible.

suggest, suggestion, suggestible   impress, impression, impressible
perfect, perfection, perfectible

These words do not take the –ible ending: accept, return, envy. What makes them different?

The generalization is _____

_____

Look back at what you have learned and list when you use –able and when you use –ible.

Now complete the following exercise, adding –able or –ible.

support_____

recover_____

work_____

compare_____

note_____

separate_____

obtain_____

respect_____

identify_____

admiss_____

comprehens_____

regret_____

profit_____

communicate_____

remove_____

excite_____

adjust_____

pleasure_____

embrace_____

unpredict_____

invis_____

indestruct_____

From course materials, I&L 2231, Teaching Language Arts in the Intermediate Grades, University of Pittsburgh, 1998.

Mystery Word

Mystery Word is an instructional strategy used primarily to promote decoding of multisyllabic words. As children begin reading more complex texts with more difficult words with multiple syllables, they need to learn that it is more efficient to figure out words by chunking their pronounceable word parts, mainly prefixes, suffixes, roots, and base words, rather than trying to decode by sounding out individual phonemes. Chunking words in this manner speeds up the reading process, whereas sounding out individual letters and sounds slows it down. Another benefit of the **Mystery Word** strategy is that it helps support the reader in learning how to spell these multisyllabic words because they have been broken down into prefixes, roots, base words, and suffixes.

The procedures for preparing for and playing Mystery Word are as follows:

Teacher Preparations

Step 1: Choose words of three or four syllables (or more) from the literature that students are reading or from the textbook being read to serve as the Mystery Word(s).

Step 2: Place short lines on a paper (or chart paper, chalkboard, etc.), one line for each letter of the Mystery Word.

Step 3: If the Mystery Word is three (3) syllables long, find three other words, **EACH** word containing **ONE** of the syllable parts of the Mystery Word. List these words in random order under the Mystery Word lines.

Step 4: Provide the list of possible questions (see below) that students can ask to determine what the Mystery Word is, using parts of the other words listed to piece together to form the Mystery Word. The possible questions are:

Does the Mystery Word begin like the word_____?
Does the Mystery Word end like the word_____?
Does the Mystery Word have a middle like the word_____?
Does the Mystery Word have a middle like the end of_____?
Does the Mystery Word begin like the middle of_____?
Does the Mystery Word end like the middle of_____?
Does the Mystery Word have a middle like the beginning of_____?

How to Play

Step 1: One at a time, children ask one of the questions above, to try to hone in on the different syllables of the Mystery Word. If a child gets a question correct, the teacher says "Yes" and writes that syllable on the appropriate lines in the Mystery Word. Then the word from the list that contains that syllable part is crossed off and not used again for this Mystery Word. If the child guesses incorrectly, the teacher says "No" and the next child asks a question. No clue word is crossed out at this time.

Step 2: As each syllable and its position in the Mystery Word has been guessed, the clue word in the list is crossed out and not used again for that Mystery Word.

Step 3: Play continues in this manner until the Mystery Word has been determined.

Example:

Mystery Word:

<u>c</u>   <u>o</u>   <u>m</u>   <u>f</u>   <u>o</u>   <u>r</u>   <u>t</u>   <u>a</u>   <u>b</u>   <u>l</u>   <u>e</u>

~~pay**able**~~
~~**com**pany~~
~~mis**fort**une~~

Questions:
Does the word end like the middle of misfortune? (No)
Does the word begin like the word company? (Yes)
Does the word have a middle like the end of payable? (No)
Does the word have a middle like misfortune? (Yes)
Does the word end like payable? (Yes)

Mystery Word:

<u>e</u>   <u>m</u>   <u>p</u>   <u>l</u>   <u>o</u>   <u>y</u>   <u>m</u>   <u>e</u>   <u>n</u>   <u>t</u>

~~de**ploy**~~
~~**em**barrass~~
~~depart**ment**~~

Questions:
Does the word begin like the middle of department? (No)
Does the word end like end of deploy? (No)
Does the word have a middle like the middle of embarrass?(No)
Does the word have a middle like the end of deploy? (Yes)
Does the word begin like the beginning of department? (No)
Does the word end like department? (Yes)
Does the word begin like the beginning of embarrass? (Yes)

Other Mystery Words and clue word set examples:

contestant
   inform**ant**
   condensation
   pre**test**ing

unprogressive
   re**gress**ion
   program
   unusual
   combat**ive**

irresistible
   imposs**ible** (keep ible together)
   restore
   in**sist**
   irrelevant

university
   immunit**y**
   di**ver**se
   sen**sit**ive
   uniform (keep uni together)

committee
   induc**tee**
   comfortable
   per**mit**

performance
   formation
   perplexing
   annoy**ance**

Adapted from: Cunningham, P.M. (1990, October). The Names Test: A quick assessment of decoding ability. *The Reading Teacher*, 44(2), 124–129. Copyright 1990 by the International Reading Association (www.reading.org)

Procedures
for Syllasearch

Syllasearch is an effective instructional strategy designed to assist readers in decoding multisyllabic words using analysis and synthesis. Roth, McKeown, and Beck (1985) designed Syllasearch from an early, out-of-use computer program. The strategy is useful for grades one and up provided that students are reading words of two or more syllables. Students enjoy Syllasearch because they perceive the activities associated with it as a game.

Syllasearch has three parts to the strategy. In the first part, **Meet the Words,** students become acquainted with the words as the teacher reads each word aloud, showing the words one at a time, asking the students to read along or repeat after you. In the second part, **Find the Syllables,** students are asked to find the syllables of the given words, and those syllables become the parts that they use to make words in the third part of the activity, **Collect the Words.** *Collect the Words* has two versions, described below. See the script and directions for each activity below:

Meet the Words:

- Display all words in a column on the chalkboard or on cards in a pocket chart.

center	cen	ket	ous
market	mar	ter	lade
marvel	bris	vel	
marvelous	chap	shal	
marshal		ma	
marmalade			
brisket			
chapter			

- Tell students that these are the words that they will use in the game.

- Go down the list, pointing to each word, reading it aloud, and for those words you don't think the students have heard before give a brief sentence or definition-like statement. For example, "Marvel. Marvel means to think something is wonderful or marvelous. Somebody might say 'I marvel at how fast a roller coaster goes.'" Do not belabor the meaning of the words. Rather, using a word in a sentence is just to provide a quick context that some students may remember.

- Assure students that if some of the words are unfamiliar now, it is all right because the game will help them learn them. Stress that an important first step in learning the words is to both hear and say them. Read the words aloud again, encouraging students to say them with you. Keep *Meet the Words* brief and fast paced. At another time you may want to come back and deal with the meanings or other aspects of the words in more depth. As an introductory phase, however, *Meet the Words* is only to provide students with a context of a "set" of words that they will deal with in a particular game of Syllasearch.

- Before beginning the next phase, *Find the Syllables,* remove the complete set of words.

Find the Syllables:

- Place the first word in the list you have selected in the pocket chart and pronounce it somewhat deliberately, asking the students to say it with you.

*"This word is **center**. Read it with me, **center**."*

- With the word still in the pocket chart, invite a student to the board to point to the parts of a word that you say, and to name the letters in the syllables.

> *"Point to the letters that make the **cen** sound in center.*
> *What are the letters that make the **cen** sound in **center**?"*

> *"Point to the letters that make the **ter** sound in center.*
> *What are the letters that make the **ter** sound in **center**?"*

- As the student points to the correct syllable, and tells you the letters, put the corresponding syllable card on the chalkboard or in a pocket chart, arranging the cards in a matrix identical to that on the Syllable Matrix for those words. For example, the syllable card 'cen' should appear at the top of the first column of the matrix. The syllable card for 'ter' should appear in the second column, second row.

cen

      ter

- Continue in this way until all the words in the list have been shown and pronounced, and all the syllable cards are arranged in the matrix.

cen	ket	ous
mar	ter	lade
bris	vel	
chap	shal	
	ma	

Note: An easy way to keep track of where the syllable cards go is to put a small code in the corner of each card, e.g., on the 'cen' card (col. 1, row 1), and on the 'ter' card, (col. 2, row 2). A pocket chart or Fun Tak is recommended for placing the syllable cards in the matrix so that they can be easily and repeatedly removed and replaced. When you get to a repeated syllable, (e.g. 'vel' will already be on the matrix when the syllables for 'marvelous' are requested), just tell the students that the syllable is already on the matrix.

- Tell the students that they now have the parts of the words and are ready to go on to the part of the game called *Collect the Words*.

Collect the Words:

- In this part of the game, students collect words by combining syllables from the matrix columns.

- There are two versions for *Collect the Words*.

Version 1

- Ask students to look at the matrix and listen to the word that you say. After you say the word, invite a student to come to the chart and build the word. You can start with any word on the list, but only say the word, you do not show the word. As indicated, the procedures go as follows:

> "Listen to the word I say. **Marvelous . . . marvelous.**"

- Invite a student to come to the chart to build the word. The student should pull away one syllable from each column to build the word, placing the syllable cards below the matrix to form the word. So the display would look like the following:

cen	ket	
	ter	lade
bris		
chap	shal	
	ma	

                marvelous

- Have the students read the word that was built from the syllables, and return each of the syllable cards in the word to their place in the matrix.

- Students can write the word, as you write the word on the chalkboard or put the completed word card (not the syllables that make the word) at the far right of the pocket chart, so that the display looks like the following:

cen	ket	ous	**marvelous**
mar	ter	lade	
bris	vel		
chap	shal		
	ma		

- Continue in the same way until all the words have been built, pronounced, and written. At the completion of this version of *Collect the Words,* the final display should look as follows, with the exception that the list of words can be in any order.

cen	ket	ous	**center**
mar	ter	lade	**market**
bris	vel		**marvel**
chap	shal		**marvelous**
	ma		**marshal**
			marmalade
			brisket
			chapter

Version 2

- This version starts with the matrix. The difference is that instead of you telling the students what word to make, as in Version 1 above, call on a student to come and make any word s/he likes, noting that there are eight real words that can be made. When a word is made, write that word on the chalkboard, or place it in the pocket chart as a way of keeping track of which of the words have been built. For example, a student comes up and says: "I can make the word '**marshal**' by taking the syllable '**mar**' and the syllable '**shal**'. That makes '**marshal**'."

Other ways of practicing:

- Have the students make their own set of syllable cards with index cards and markers.

- Using the matrix on the board as a model, students can arrange the cards in the same formation on their desks and try to build the eight words. They can check their success with the list of words they wrote in version 1.

- Working in pairs, ask the students to make some words with the syllables, both real and nonsense words, pronounce them to their partners, and then write them.

- There are a variety of game-like "overlays" that can be applied to Syllasearch, such as keeping track of how fast a student or a pair of students can build all of the words, etc. The important point is repeated practice of finding the syllables (which is analysis of words) and then collecting the words (which is synthesis of words) which will help students tackle new multisyllabic words. It is important, however, that the repeated practices be fun. If they get boring and too pedantic, they lose their potential power.

These procedures were adapted in January, 1996, from a computer program developed in 1985 by Isabel Beck, Steven Roth, & Margaret McKeown. The original computer program was distributed by Developmental Learning Materials, Allen, Texas.

Sets of Words and Syllables for Syllasearch

Some easy words

	Words	Syllables	
1.	barber	mo	tom
	bottle	shal	lor
	stupid	bar	tion
	circus	par	cus
	motion	bot	dent
	pillow	stu	low
	student	stu	ber
	parlor	pil	pid
	shallow	cir	tle

	Words	Syllables	
2.	below	be	board
	apple	fan	dent
	capture	be	ple
	cupboard	cap	ty
	indent	par	low
	beware	bar	cy
	party	in	ware
	barter	par	ter
	fancy	cup	ture

Some medium words

	Words	Syllables		
1.	suddenly	vis	i	ing
	another	hid	ter	er
	hidden	mas	oth	ful
	helpfully	sud	ful	ble
	powerful	vis	er	ly
	visible	pic	fer	tor
	picture	suf	den	
	visitor	an	ture	
	suffering	help	l	
	master	pow	den	

	Words	Syllables		
2.	principal	na	ma	dent
	princess	bris	ci	ous
	accident	prin	shal	pal
	marvelous	chap	ket	lade
	marmalade	ac	cess	
	chapter	mar	tion	
	nation	prin	ter	
	marshal	ac	vel	
	action	mar	tion	
	brisket	mar	ma	

Some hard words

	Words	Syllables			
1.	protective	ac	tac	tive	lar
	reverse	con	sult	sa	tion
	advertise	pro	di	tise	
	conversation	con	gan	u	
	spectacular	re	com	dent	
	accomplish	au	tec	plish	
	confident	con	ver	tic	
	gigantic	ad	fi	tion	
	audition	gi	verse	ant	
	consultant	spec	ver		

	Words	Syllables			
2.	mattress	de	then	tion	ble
	tradition	re	ves	pa	ny
	deceivable	in	form	ma	cate
	accompany	mat	tress	tive	gate
	authenticate	de	tec	a	tion
	detective	tra	com	a	
	investigate	au	ceiv	ti	
	reformation	ac	di	ti	

Compiled from samples listed on Course Handout Materials from computer program developed in 1985 by: Beck, I., Roth, S., & McKeown, M. (1996). *Procedures for Syllasearch.* Allen, TX: Developmental Learning Materials.

Elements of Fluency

Fluency involves much more than just how fast and accurate a person reads. It also involves **prosody**, which is the variation in loudness, pitch, rhythm, pause, and speed that provides the spoken equivalent of the written text. When considering reading **rate**, or speed, one measures the number of words per minute a child reads aloud. **Accuracy** refers to the number of miscues made while reading aloud during a measured length of time, normally one minute.

The following relate to **prosodic features** (also used for stress):

- pitch: high or low tone
- loudness: soft or loud voice
- speed: fast or slow speed
- pause: short or long pause

The following relate to **paralinguistic** features:

- whisper: for secrecy
- breathiness: for emotion
- huskiness: for disparagement
- nasality: for anxiety or sarcasm
- over articulation: for exaggeration

The following are examples of **prosodic and paralinguistic** features:

- clipped: "No, don't bother me again." (angry, impatient)
- elongated: "No, but I could change my mind." (hesitant, unsure)
- louder: "No, I will not!" (defiant, definite)
- softer: "No, I'm sorry." (apologetic)
- pause: "No . . . why not?" (questioning)
- even pitch: "Please say 'yes' or 'no'." (informative)
- high pitch: "No, you are not getting married." (delight, excitement)
- low pitch: "No, not in this class." (authoritative)
- whisper: "No, don't tell anyone." (secrecy)
- nasality: "No, that's not my sister." (childish, sarcastic)
- breathiness: "No, I can't do that." "I'm sorry." (emotional)
- lip rounding: "No, baby can't have that." (talk to infant or pet)

From *The Reading Teacher's Book of Lists,* 5th edition by E.B. Fry and J.E. Kress. Reprinted by permission of John Wiley & Sons.

How Punctuation Relates to Comprehension and Fluency

Without **punctuation**, readers would have difficulty comprehending what they read. Punctuation supports fluency which, in turn, aids in understanding the text because it serves as "road signs," telling when the reader needs to pause, when to raise and drop his voice, and when to read with emotion. Each punctuation symbol provides information that assists the reader as he adjusts his pace, makes pauses, and adjusts his intonation. Listed below are punctuation marks with explanations for how they support fluency and comprehension.

The **period** (.) is most important for prosody. Readers must give a generous pause for periods at the end of sentences to denote the end of a complete thought.

The **comma**'s (,) length of pause is less than that for a period but long enough to allow the reader and/or listener to determine a break between items in a series, between clauses, or appositives and context clues (Jack, the boy next door; We saw a pod, a group of dolphins, in the water.)

The **question mark** (?) shows that a question is being asked; therefore, most often a rising pitch toward the end of the sentence takes place, followed by a major pause.

An **exclamation point** (!) indicates a strong emotion or definite thought pattern taking place. Therefore the reader should increase the loudness of his voice, especially near the end of the sentence. Other prosodic features can also be used to indicate stress.

A **semicolon** (;) is not used as frequently as a comma or period, but the reader should pause for a length of time somewhere between what he does for commas and periods. For oral reading, a **colon** (:) is treated like a semicolon with regard to length of pause.

Quotation marks (" ") usually indicate spoken dialogue, which tells the oral reader to change voice and use paralinguistic features such as whisper or breathiness. Quotation marks are also used to bring attention to a word, title, or phrase. Therefore, the reader can use any of the stressing techniques of prosodic features, like changing pitch or speed.

Parentheses ( ) are stronger than commas for setting off parenthetical material. They require a longer pause than a comma, both before and after the word or words they contain. Words within the parentheses can also be spoken differently from the rest of the words in the sentence, using prosodic and paralinguistic features.

The **hyphen** (-) between two words joins the words, often making them a compound word. As a result, this joining makes a them compound word. Note the difference between "a man eating lobster" and "a man-eating lobster". The hyphen decreases any pause of juncture between words.

A **dash** (—) is printed longer than a hyphen. It separates parts of a sentence and sometimes makes a separate sentence. When reading orally, the reader should pause for the same length of time as he would for a period.

An **ellipsis** (. . .) designates that a change of thought is taking place, a lapse of time, or incomplete thought. The reader must pause for the same length of time as he would for a period or dash.

From *The Reading Teacher's Book of Lists*, 5th edition by E.B. Fry and J.E. Kress. Reprinted by permission of John Wiley & Sons.

Methods and Activities for Teaching Fluency

There are ways a teacher can provide fluency practice for students. However, one of the best things a teacher can do to help improve students' fluency is to model how to read various types of texts, then have students reread it with the teacher, as they attempt to imitate the teacher's intonation, speed, and prosodic features. Be sure that students are reading texts that are at their instructional level when assessing fluency. Activities to engage students in to foster fluency are as follows:

Repeated Readings: Engage students in rereading a short selection or passage several times to try to increase speed, accuracy, and prosody. Use a tape recorder to record each student's progress.

Decoding by Chunking Word Parts: Teach students to decode by looking at morphemes and inflectional endings (word parts such as prefixes, base or root words, and suffixes) rather than sounding out individual phonemes. This speeds up the word identification process and helps students read more smoothly.

Dramatic Reading: Engage students in practicing oral reading of parts for a play, radio drama, or for the dialogue in prose (narratives). Encourage them to read with prosodic and paralinguistic features in mind.

Vocabulary Development: Focus on vocabulary instruction to teach the meaning and pronunciation of unfamiliar words. As a result, students will read with more confidence and fluency.

Punctuation Instruction: Teach the importance of how punctuation impacts fluency and comprehension. Model and invite students to read along.

Reader's Theatre: Engaging students in reader's theatre provides a venue for children to practice their oral reading skills in an interesting way. Students either choose a scene from a book they've read or rewrite a story they've read, then choose parts. After some rehearsal, they read from the text or rewritten parts as they "perform" their parts. No costuming or dramatic acting is necessary. Students just read their parts with proper prosodic and paralinguistic features.

Choral Reading: Put students into groups. Divide reading passages and assign groups to passages to read chorally. This activity works very well with poetry.

Author's Chair: As children write during writing workshop, they read aloud a story or piece of writing they are working on to get feedback from their classmates.

Formal Speech: Students write speeches for various reasons and read them to the class or other audiences.

Radio Program: Small group takes parts and reads a radio script into a tape recorder to present to the class or parent group.

Joke of the Day: Each day, a given student reads a joke or funny story to the class.

Official Announcer: Each day a different student is chosen to read announcements, short selections, student writings, bulletins, etc. The announcer may practice/prepare in advance.

From *The Reading Teacher's Book of Lists,* 5th edition by E.B. Fry and J.E. Kress. Reprinted by permission of John Wiley & Sons.

Practice with Sentence Intonation

Changing the emphasis on one word in any given sentence can have a major impact on the meaning of the sentence. The changes in meaning are due to what is called *supersegmental* phonemes. A phoneme is the smallest unit of sound and a *supersegmental* phoneme is one that has an additional change to the typical phoneme, that is, a change in inflection or stress, that affects meaning. Teachers must instruct students about the importance of this characteristic of English because it aids in comprehension of both spoken and written language.

Directions: Read the sentences below, emphasizing or stressing the bold word to change the meaning of the sentence.

I did not see her take your purse.   [Someone else saw her take it.]

I **did** not see her take your purse.   [Indignant denial of seeing someone take it.]

I did **not** see her take your purse.   [Strong denial of seeing someone taking it.]

I did not **see** her take your purse.   [I implied it was taken, but I didn't see it taken.]

I did not see **her** take your purse.   [I didn't see that particular girl take it.]

I did not see her **take** your purse.   [That particular girl I saw didn't take the purse. She may have *moved* it, but didn't *take* it.]

I did not see her take **your** purse.   [That particular girl took someone else's purse.]

I did not see her take your **purse.**   [That girl took something else of yours, but not your purse.]

Try the same shifting of emphasis with these sentences and discuss each one.

Jim did not lose Tom's homework.

You were not invited to Sue's party.

George did not give me ten dollars.

From *The Reading Teacher's Book of Lists,* 5th edition by E.B. Fry and J.E. Kress. Reprinted by permission of John Wiley & Sons.

Appendix

Syllabication Generalizations

There has been some controversy regarding whether or not to teach syllabication rules in elementary school. The way words are divided into syllables affects the way vowels are pronounced in open and closed syllables. Rather than teach "rules" of syllabication, only to confuse children when having to present exceptions to the rules, preference is given to using the term "generalizations" because the term implies that there may be exceptions.

Generalization #1: **VCV**
A vowel-consonant-vowel pattern will generally be divided after the consonant unless the first vowel is long
[wag-on   bro-ken   pres-ent   me-ter]

Generalization #2: **VCCV**
Divide between the two consonants unless the consonants are a digraph
[mas-ter   hun-ter   weath-er   ush-er]

Generalization #3: **VCCCV**
In words with three consonants between two vowels, divide between the blend or digraph and the other consonant
[an-gler   mon-ster]

Generalization #4: **Affixes**

1. *Prefixes* are always separate syllables
   [re-bound, un-for-tun-ate]

2. *Suffixes* form separate syllables if they contain a vowel sound
   [hap-pi-ness, mouth-ful]

3. The suffix –*y* tends to pick up the preceding consonant to form a separate syllable.
   [light-ly, taste-ful-ly]

4. The *inflectional ending* –*ed* tends to form a separate syllable only when it follows a base word or root that ends in *d* or *t*.
   [plant-ed, start-ed, but not in stopped]

5. The *inflectional ending* –*s* **only** forms a syllable when it follows an *e*. Otherwise, the –s ending will not be a syllable in itself.
   [at-oms, cours-es]

Generalization #5: **Compounds**	Divide compound words between the words [bath-tub arm-band] In compound words that have multiple syllables within the words, divide first between the words, then divide the words accordingly. [weather-man becomes weath-er-man]
Generalization #6: **Final *le***	Final *le* takes on the consonant that comes immediately before it to form a syllable [la-ble nim-ble crum-ble]
Generalization #7: **Vowels**	Do not split common vowel blends, clusters, digraphs, and diphthongs, such as: 1. Long vowel digraphs (ee, ea, ai, oa, ow, ie) [crea-ture] 2. R-controlled vowels (ar, er, ir, or, ur) [par-ti-cle, fur-ni-ture] 3. Diphthongs (oi, oy, ou, ow) [a-void-ance, thou-sand] 4. Double *o* like *oo* [soon, took] 5. Broad *o* clusters (au, aw, al) [au-di-ence, aw-ful, al-right]
Generalization #8: **Vowel Problems**	For every syllable, there must be only one vowel sound. Therefore, there will be as many syllables in a word as there are vowel sounds (vowel phonemes). 1. The letter *e* at the end of a word is generally silent. 2. The letter *y* at the end or in the middle of a word works like a vowel (sounds like a long *e* or long *i*). If a *y* comes at the beginning of a word, it works like a consonant. [sky, mon-key, ver-y, cy-cle, yel-low, yak] 3. Two vowels together that make separate sounds form separate syllables. [po-li-o, i-de-a]

From *The Reading Teacher's Book of Lists,* 5th edition by E.B. Fry and J.E. Kress. Reprinted by permission of John Wiley & Sons.

Some Spelling "Rules" (Generalizations)

"Rules"/Generalizations for Adding Affixes (inflectional endings, suffixes)

- **For the most part,** to change a verb form, change a word to an adverb, compare an adjective, or make a word plural, simply add the affix! Some examples are:

  spell + s (spells)   spell + ing (spelling)   spell + ed (spelled)
  small + er (smaller)   small + est (smallest)   slow + ly (slowly)
  book + s (books)   car + s (cars)   bucket + s (buckets)

- **For words that end in 'e'. . .**

  - drop the final 'e' if the affix begins with a vowel.
    (nose—nosy; quote—quotable; tame—tamed; dine—dining)
  - keep the final 'e' if the affix begins with a consonant.
    (desperate—desperately; care—careless; hope—hopeful; complete—completeness)
  - keep the final 'e' if it is preceded by a vowel.
    (flee—fleeing; see—seeing; dye—dyeing [the y serves as a vowel in this word]

- **For words that end in 'y'. . .**

  - change the 'y' to 'i' if the 'y' is preceded by a consonant.
    (marry—married; bury—buries; lady—ladies; merry—merrily)
  - keep the 'y' if it is preceded by a vowel.
    (joy—joyous; boy—boyish)
  - keep the 'y' if the affix begins with 'i'.
    (marry—marrying; carry—carrying; copy—copying)

- **For words that end in 'c'. . .**

  - add a 'k' before an affix that begins with an 'e', 'i', or 'y'.
    (picnic—picnicking; panic—panicky)

- **For words that end in a single consonant . . .**

  - if the one-syllable word ends in a consonant or has a final accented syllable, double the final consonant. (drag—dragged; bus—bussed) Exception: perplex—perplexed
  - if the word ends in two consonants, the last consonant is not doubled. (hand—handed, handy; spark—sparked, sparks, sparking)
  - if the word contains a single vowel, double the final consonant, but if it has a two-letter vowel phoneme, do not double the consonant. (run—running, runner; rain—rained, rainy)
  - if the word ends in a single consonant and the affix begins with a vowel, double the consonant. (beg—begged, begging)
  - if the word ends in 'le' and the affix is 'ly', drop the final 'le' before adding the affix (able— ably), but if the word ends in 'l', leave the 'l' before adding 'ly'. (cool—coolly)

From *The Reading Teacher's Book of Lists,* 5th edition by E.B. Fry and J.E. Kress. Reprinted by permission of John Wiley & Sons.

"Rules"/Generalizations for Forming Plurals

- Most nouns are made plural by adding *-s* to the end of the word.

  goat—goats   place—places   task—tasks
  step—steps   leg—legs   table—tables

- Words that end in **y** that are preceded by a consonant will form the plural by changing the **y** to **i** and adding **es**.

  city—cities   country—countries   fairy—fairies
  family—families   party—parties   county—counties

- Words that end in *-s, -ss, -sh, -ch, -x,* or *-z* form the plural by adding *-es*.

  lass—lasses   lash—lashes   lunch—lunches
  fox—foxes   waltz—waltzes   fax—faxes

- Words that end in a **y** followed by a vowel form the plural by adding *-s*.

  monkey—monkeys   turkey—turkeys   play—plays
  cay—cays   stray—strays   toy—toys

- Some nouns that end in *-f* or *-fe* are formed by adding *-s*.

  cliff—cliffs   belief—beliefs   gulf—gulfs
  cuff—cuffs   roof—roofs

- Most nouns that end in *-f* or *-fe* are formed by changing the *-f* to *-v* and adding *-es*.

  leaf—leaves   knife—knives   elf—elves
  thief—thieves   wolf—wolves   life—lives
  self—selves   half—halves   wife—wives

- Words that end in *-o* that's preceded by a consonant form the plural by adding *-es*.

  tomato—tomatoes   echo—echoes   zero—zeroes
  hero—heroes   cargo—cargoes   potato—potatoes

- Words that end in *-o* that's preceded by a vowel form the plural by adding *-s*.

  video—videos   radio—radios   patio—patios

- Compound words form their plurals by making the base noun plural. So first, determine what the base noun is, then determine the "rule" for making the base noun plural.

  brother-in-law—**brothers**-in-law   sand**box**—sand**boxes**   **passer**by—**passers**by
  head**light**—head**lights**   **attorney** general—**attorneys** general

---

From *The Reading Teacher's Book of Lists,* 5th edition by E.B. Fry and J.E. Kress. Reprinted by permission of John Wiley & Sons.

- Of course, there are many words that have irregular plural forms. These must be memorized. Wide reading and writing will help students learn them.

child—children	radius—radii	ox—oxen	die—dice
louse—lice	man—men	woman—women	basis—bases
goose—geese	crisis—crises	stimulus—stimuli	index—indices
medium—media	axis—axes	criterion—criteria	oasis—oases
foot—feet	parenthesis—parentheses	appendix—appendices	tooth—teeth
datum—data	mouse—mice		

- There are some words in which their singular forms and are plural forms are spelled the same.

cod	moose	species	hay	sheep	gross	rye
deer	music	wheat	Swiss	British	trout	bass
series	corps	traffic	barley	dirt	aircraft	fish
salmon	mackerel	dozen				

- Some words are singular even though they may look plural.

people	folk	cattle	livestock	police	vermin

- Collective nouns imply more than one; however, when used in a sentence, they are treated as a singular noun when used as the subject of the sentence.

Mrs. Smith's <u>class</u> is singing *New York, New York* in the school musical. (class of students)
The <u>army</u> is fighting the battle and to win the war. (army of soldiers)
The <u>herd</u> runs freely across the prairie. (dozens of horses)
The <u>gaggle</u> is chasing the dog around the barnyard. (group of geese)
The British <u>flotilla (fleet)</u> is aimed at confronting the Spanish <u>armada.</u> (groups of ships)
The tired mother gathered her <u>brood</u> and sent them off to school. (group of children or chickens)
The new <u>faculty</u> in our school is going to add an exciting dimension to teaching this year! (group of teachers)

Other collective nouns:

association (of professionals)	convention (of professionals)
audience (of listeners)	corps (of marines)
band (of gorillas, jays, musicians, robbers)	council (of advisors)
bevy (of ladies, swans, quail)	crew (of sailors, workers)
bundle (of clothes, money, sticks)	culture (of bacteria)
cast (of actors)	grove (of trees)
chain (of islands)	murder (of crows)
chorus (of singers)	network (of computers)
club (of members)	pack (of dogs, hounds, lies, wolves)
collection (of stamps, books, coins, art)	range (of mountains)
congress (of delegates)	swarm (of bees, reporters)
colony (of ants, people, writers, artists)	troupe (of performers)
committee (of people)	union (of employees)
company (of firefighters, soldiers, workers)	wealth (of information)

From *The Reading Teacher's Book of Lists,* 5th edition by E.B. Fry and J.E. Kress. Reprinted by permission of John Wiley & Sons.